EVANGELINE N. ASAFOR PHD

# GRATITUDE TO GODLY PRAYERS THE LADDER TO GODLY SUCCESS

## GODLY PRAYERS

Gratitude to Godly Prayers the Ladder to Godly Success
Godly Prayers
All Rights Reserved.
Copyright © 2021 Evangeline N. Asafor PhD
v2.0

The opinions expressed in this manuscript are solely the opinions of the author and do not represent the opinions or thoughts of the publisher. The author has represented and warranted full ownership and/or legal right to publish all the materials in this book.

This book may not be reproduced, transmitted, or stored in whole or in part by any means, including graphic, electronic, or mechanical without the express written consent of the publisher except in the case of brief quotations embodied in critical articles and reviews.

Paperback ISBN: 978-1-64999-180-5

Cover Photo © 2021 Evangeline N. Asafor, Ph.D All rights reserved - used with permission.

Grateful Soul LLC and the "Grateful Soul" logo are trademarks belonging to Grateful Soul LLC

PRINTED IN THE UNITED STATES OF AMERICA

# Dedication

*This Godly inspired book is dedicated to all the modern day current and future Abrahams, Daniels, Davids, Esthers, Elijah, Hannahs, Jeremiahs, Josephs, Joshuas, Moses, Nehemiahs, Noahs the Naomis. These men and women of the Bible throughout scripture did not appear successful in the eyes of society but were obedient to God and in due time they were favored tremendously and used to show case the goodness of God. To all who are reading this book, may your purpose-driven lives be transformed into mission-accomplished lives of Godly success in Jesus Name Amen!*

# About the Author

**Dr. Evangeline Asafor** Ngwashi is a self -motivated, result-driven, and innovative professional with advanced knowledge in nonprofit management, leadership development, business management, and criminal justice. Dr. Ngwashi currently serves on the executive board of the proposed Hebrews Federal Credit Union as the Director of Compliance for the State of Florida. She is an Advisory Board Member for QualityMD, Funders USA and College Food Network. From the healthcare perspective, Dr. Ngwashi has experience in Hospice Care, Geriatric Care, and Home Health Nursing. Dr. Ngwashi holds five degrees in Law and Business including a Doctorate Degree in Criminal Justice and painstakingly conducted a novel research project on Financial Accountability in U.S Nonprofit Organizations. As an author, Dr. Ngwashi has published five books with an astounding global readership. As a motivational speaker, Dr. Ngwashi has provided tremendous value to the multitude that have been opportuned to hear her.

*"I am a Champion of HOPE. My special gift from God is the*

*gift of Hope. My purpose in life is to play an essential role in other people's lives by helping them to accept the idea that they can work with God to fully realize their purpose on earth. I laugh even if sometimes I am sad. My smile could brighten anyone's day! I am caring and giving even if sometimes I am Exhausted.*

*I face struggles with strength and courage. I never give up and I know that no matter what, I can always make it through by God's grace and according to his WILL for my life. I have embraced my Godly given assignment, anointing, and empowerment with a grateful heart and a humble spirit. Like Samson the great Bible warrior, I am blessed with immense strength, though not physical. Even in moments when I feel like all my strength is completed depleted, I still find a way to do what needs to be done.*

*I praise God because I am fearfully and wonderfully made in God's own image and my life is sacred. I am a masterpiece, an original, handpicked by God, and I am a person of extreme value and significance. I have inherited my maternal grandmother's generosity and warmth, My father's bravery and determination and my mother's passion and loyalty.*

*I give hope to others and enable them to envision a better future thus motivating them to take steps to make it happen. I give hope through motivation, acts of compassion and kindness, acts of love, acts of forgiveness, acts of empowerment. I give hope by living my life in such a way that those who do not know God will come to know HIM because they know me.*

*I am who God says I am, I can do what God says I can do, and I will become all what God wants me to become in Jesus Name, Amen."*

# Table of Contents

| | |
|---|---|
| Introduction | i |
| 1. What is a Prayer | 1 |
| 2. Why Do We Pray? | 5 |
| 3. What is a Godly Prayer? | 13 |
| 4. When You Pray, Hold God in Remembrance of His Promises | 16 |
| 5. The Promise of the Holy Spirit by Jesus Christ | 27 |
| 6. Praying in an Unknown Tongue | 33 |
| 7. The Special Role of Forgiveness in Godly Prayers | 38 |
| 8. The Crucial Role of Gratitude in Godly Prayers | 43 |
| 9. The Crucial Role of Fasting in Godly Prayers | 47 |
| 10. God's will for Our Lives | 51 |
| 11. When you Pray, Pray According to God's Will | 60 |
| 12. When We Pray, We Must Praise God by Singing | 63 |
| 13. We Must Pray Without Ceasing | 66 |
| 14. Patience as the Greatest Prayer | 69 |
| 15. Fourteen Steps to Praying a Godly Prayer | 72 |
| 16. How Does God Answer our Prayers? | 80 |
| 17. The Role of the Holy Spirit in our Prayer Lives | 84 |
| 18. What is Godly Success? | 90 |
| 19. The Godly Prayer and Godly Success of Hannah the prophetess | 98 |
| 20. The Godly Prayer and Godly Success of Moses | 101 |
| 21. The Godly Prayer and Godly Success of Noah | 103 |
| 22. The Godly Prayer and Godly Success of Abraham | 105 |
| 23. The Godly Prayer and Godly Success of Daniel | 107 |
| 24. The Godly Prayer and Godly Success of David | 110 |

25. The Godly Prayer and Godly Success of Esther     113
26. The Godly Prayer and Godly
    Success of Nehemiah                              115
27. The Godly Prayer and Godly Success of Elijah     117
28. The Godly Prayers and Godly Success of Job       120
29. The Godly Prayers and Godly
    Success of Jeremiah                              122
30. The Godly Prayer and Godly Success of Joshua     125
31. The Godly Prayers and Godly Success of Naomi     128
32. The Godly Prayers and Godly Success of Jesus     131
33. Godly success comes at a Cost and for a Cause!   142
34. Let Jesus Christ be the Compass for our Lives!   150
35. Conclusion                                       153
    SPECIAL ACKNOWLEDGEMENT                          155
    Other Books from the Gratitude Series            157
    References                                       165

# Introduction

**MY PRAYER TO GOD ALMIGHTY IN THE NAME OF JESUS CHRIST**

**DEAR LORD, I** come before you on bended knees with a grateful heart and a humble spirit. I Love you; I worship you and I adore you. May your name be glorified! Lord, I surrender my will to your will! May your WILL be done in my life According to thy words, intentions, love, and legacy in Christ Jesus! May your words continue to communicate your Intentions for my life, may your intentions continue to be about your love for me! May your love continue to guarantee my legacy in Christ Jesus! And may my legacy in Christ Jesus lead me to life everlasting! Amen!

    Father thank you for blessing me with the special gift of HOPE! Thank you for a future filled with hope and prosperity **(Jeremiah 29:11)** Thank you that my path gets brighter and brighter **(Proverbs 4:18)**. Thanks for making me a happy mother of children **(Psalm 113:9).**

    Thank you that the fruit of my womb is blessed. Thank you that my children will rise and call me blessed **(Deuteronomy 28:4).** Thank you that my children will be mighty in the land **(Psalm 112:2)**. Thank you that with long life you will satisfy me! **(Psalm 91:16)**. Thank you that my latter days will be better than my former days **(Job 42:12)**. Lord, thank you that I will not die but live, and will proclaim what you have done **(Psalm 118:17)**.

My Father, my God, thank you for bestowing on me a crown of beauty instead of ashes, the oil of joy instead of mourning, and a garment of praise instead of a spirit of despair**(Isaiah 61:3)**. My Lord, thank you for opening the heavens, the storehouse of your bounty, sending rain on my land in season and blessing all the work of my hands Thank you that I will lend and not borrow**(Deuteronomy 28:12)**. Thank you that the enemies I see today, I shall never see again **(Exodus 14:13)**. Thanks for being my vindicator and for assuring me that no weapon fashioned against me shall prevail **(Isaiah 54:17)**. Thank you that your favor upon my life is not for a season but for a lifetime **(Psalm 30:5)**.

Thanks for always making a way for me even where there seems to be no way **(Isaiah 43:19)**. Thank you for forgiving me, for not counting my sins and for reconciling me to yourself in Christ**(Corinthians 5:18-19)**.Thank you for being good , doing good and for teaching me your decrees **(Psalm 119:68)**.Thanks for assuring me that you will be with me constantly until you give me all what you promised**(Genesis 28:15)**.

Where you lead me, I will follow, when you call me, I will answer, please help show me your ways! Deliver me from all that is evil Lord **(2 Timothy 4:18)**. Lord may every word that comes out of my mouth, and every meditation in my heart, be acceptable in thy holy and mighty presence! May every knee bow and every thought confess at the mention of your name **(Isaiah 45:23)**. Help me to live in such a way that those who know me but do not know you, will come to know you because they know me. Forgive me my sins and help me to be swift in forgiving those who sin against me.

Thank you that my children and I are fearfully and wonderfully made! Thank you that I am blessed and anointed! Thank you that I am strong, capable, and efficient! Thank you that I am prosperous! Thank you that I am healed! Thank you that I am who you say I am! Thank you that I will become who you want me to become! Thank you that I can do all what you say I can do! Thank you for my family and friends, continue to bless, protect, and provide for them!

ABBA Father, I am your vessel, please use me to change whatever needs change in this world! Speak through me, love through me, sing through me, preach through me, heal through me, deliver through me, provide through me, and forgive through me! I rebuke every plan of the enemy upon the lives of my children, my friends, my family members and upon my life! By faith I declare favor upon my children, my family, my friends and upon my life.

All these I pray in Jesus Name, Amen!

## Chapter One
# WHAT IS A PRAYER

**WHAT IS A Prayer?** - Prayer as I have grown to understand and believe is a sincere appeal for help or expression of thanks directed to God almighty or a demand by faith for action or no action addressed to a situation. Prayer is the key to unlocking every door into our Godly ordained destinies. To Christians, Prayer requires a living faith in God through Christ Jesus. As described by Rev. Fr. Dr. James Urien, Prayer is more of a response to God's presence than an attempt to contact God.

Prayer is not just words that operate automatically by articulation. Prayer is not asking. Prayer is putting oneself in the hands of God, at His disposition, and listening to His voice in the depth of our hearts." (Mother Teresa). Prayer is an interaction of faith. The journey to spiritual perfection is a progressive passage from the lower to the higher stages of prayer, from ascetical to mystical prayer (St. Teresa).

Praying to God is not an option, like oxygen, praying is needed for our everyday living. Praying is a command from God! And while "praying without ceasing" (1

Thessalonians 16-18) is a command of God, the Spirit of God himself enables and empowers his people to pray. As explained by Dr. Myles Munroe, Prayer is a private affair between God and man (Jesus always prayed alone). It is God receiving a license from man to intervene on planet earth. It is therefore not a ministry for the few, it is a necessity for all. Time spent in prayer is therefore invested time and never wasted time! We must learn how to pray and teach our children and others how to pray ( Teaching them how to pray was the only thing the apostles asked Jesus to teach them how to do!).

### THERE ARE TWO TYPES OF PRAYERS: PRAYERS OF SUPPLICATION AND PRAYERS OF DECLARATION

**Job 22:27-28:** Thou shalt make thy prayer unto him, and he shall hear thee, and thou shalt pay thy vows. Thou shalt also decree a thing, and it shall be established unto thee: and the light shall shine upon thy ways.

The prayers of supplication are directed to God almighty and the prayers of declaration are directed by faith to a situation. In the holy bible, the great men and women of God prayed both prayers of supplication and prayers of declaration.

**Prayers of Supplication.** These are requests or petitions humbly presented before God almighty with an expectation that He will answer them as soon as possible. Trusting God should be at the heart of every prayer of supplication. Trust God because he created you and knows you by name (Isaiah 43:1). Trust God to hear your prayers because he is always with you (Mathew 28:20). Trust God to listen to your prayers and respond accordingly because he will fight for you (Exodus 14:14). When you pray, trust God to protect you because he is your refuge(Psalm 62:6-8).Trust God when you pray for direction because he has a plan for you (Jeremiah 29:11). Pray with confidence and trust God because he thinks about you (Psalm 139:17).

**Mathew 6:9-13**: "Our Father in heaven, hallowed be your name, your kingdom come, your will be done, on earth as it is in heaven. Give us today our daily bread. And forgive us our debts, as we also have forgiven our debtors. And lead us not into temptation but deliver us from the evil one."

**Luke 23:33-34:** When they came to the place called the Skull, they crucified him there, along with the criminals-one on his right, the other on his left. Jesus said, "Father, forgive them, for they do not know what they are doing." And they divided up his clothes by casting lots.

**Job 30:20**: I cry unto thee, and thou dost not hear me: I stand up, and thou regardest me *not*.

**Psalm 17:1:** A prayer of David. Hear me, LORD, my plea is just; listen to my cry. Hear my prayer—it does not rise from deceitful lips.

**Prayers of Declaration** These are commands sternly or fiercely directed by faith to a situation with an expectation that they will be answered as soon as possible.

**Mark 11: 22-24**: 'Have faith in God," Jesus answered. Truly I tell you, if anyone says to this mountain, 'Go, throw yourself into the sea,' and does not doubt in their heart but believes that what they say will happen, it will be done for them. Therefore, I tell you, whatever you ask for in prayer, believe that you have received it, and it will be yours."

**Luke 4:33-35:** In the synagogue there was a man possessed by a demon, an impure spirit. He cried out at the top of his voice, "Go away! What do you want with us, Jesus of Nazareth? Have you come to destroy us? I know who you are-the Holy One of God!" "Be quiet!" Jesus said sternly. "Come out of him!" Then the demon threw the man down before them all and came out without injuring him.

**James 5:17-18:** Elijah was a human being, even as we are. He prayed earnestly that it would not rain, and it did not rain on the land for three and a half years. Again, he prayed, and the heavens gave rain, and the earth produced its crops.

*Chapter Two*

# WHY DO WE PRAY?

**THE INTRIGUING AND** meaningful question "Why do we pray?" is a question most children ask and even some adults do ask. As a little girl growing up in Akum village in Cameroon near the west coast of central Africa, I asked the same question to my parent's numerous times! It was not easy for me as a child to understand why I had to constantly pray to someone I did not know, ever heard from or have ever seen! But when my earthly father referred to him as Heavenly Father and said praying to him was mandated because it was a command, I trusted my luminary Papa, a man I could see, touch, and hear!

My luminary Papa had mandates of his own for us his children and failure to follow the commands always came with serious consequences! Thus, as a child I understood early enough that if the Heavenly Father was greater than my luminary Papa, then I was better off obeying His command of praying. Consequently, I prayed more as a child out of fear for consequences than anything else.

When my Luminary Papa died in 1988 when I was barely a teenager, I had to draw closer to my Heavenly

Father for comfort and protection! But as an adult I prayed because of my love for God and His ways, my reverence of Him and as a show of gratitude to God. Prayer has since become my way of getting closer to my Heavenly Father and getting to know him better every day!

**Eleven Reasons Why we pray**

1. **We pray because it is a command from God.** God orders us to pray continually (**1 Thessalonian 5:17**). Jesus told his disciples a parable to show them that they should always pray and not give up (**Luke 18:1**). God orders us to pray because it is good and acceptable in the sight and he wants all people to be saved and to come to a knowledge of the truth (**1 Timothy 2:3-4**).
2. **Prayer is a platform for spiritual growth and total transformation.** Prayer is very vital in our spiritual walk with God from crawling, to baby steps to walking and then running in the spirit! Prayer enables us to grow in grace and increase our understanding of Jesus and to develop a close and intimate relationship with God through Christ Jesus. Prayer develops believers in wisdom and power to conform to God's standards of righteousness and his will for our lives. Prayer enables us to grow and be spiritually matured to serve God with deep devotion and reverence.
3. Prayer as a platform for growth and transformation means we must pray for spiritual hunger. This was Davids prayer for spiritual hunger "As the deer pants for streams of water, so my soul pants for you, my God. My soul thirsts for God, for the living God.

When can I go and meet with God?" **(Psalm 42:1-2)**. About eight days after Jesus said this, he took Peter, John, and James with him and went up onto a mountain to pray. As he was praying, the appearance of his face changed, and his clothes became as bright as a flash of lightning **(Luke 9:28-29)**.

4. **We pray because it is a way of enabling the Holy Spirit to transmit God's will for our lives from God's heart to our minds.** When we were saved, Christ sent the holy spirit to come dwell in the deepest, innermost part of our being. This was the beginning of God's filling us. The Holy spirit with us has the unique ability to contain God, contact God, and receive God. The Holy Spirit prays for us with God's will in mind. And he who searches our hearts knows the mind of the Spirit, because the Spirit intercedes for God's people in accordance with the will of God **(Romans 8:27)**. But you, dear friends, by building yourselves up in your most holy faith and praying in the Holy Spirit, keep yourselves in God's love as you wait for the mercy of our LORD Jesus Christ to bring you to eternal life **(Jude 1:20-21)**.

5. **We pray to show our gratitude to God.** We show God our gratitude through conversation with Him and praising him in prayers. When we pray to God, we are showing that we value our relationship with Him. It shows Him we want to tell Him everything about our days and that what He has to say is important to us. All this is for your benefit, so that the grace that is reaching more and more people may cause thanksgiving to overflow to the glory of God **(2 Corinthians 4:15)**. You will be enriched in

every way so that you can be generous on every occasion, and through us your generosity will result in thanksgiving to God **(2 Corinthians 9:11).** When you call on God to rescue you in time of trouble, he promises to deliver you, and ask for you to honor him **(Psalm 50:15).** When you pray, give thanks to God with all your heart and tell of all his wonderful deeds **(Psalm 9:1).** When you pray, give shouts of grateful praise to God **(Jonah 2:9).** Enter his gates with thanksgiving and his courts with praise; give thanks to him and praise his name **(Psalm 100:4).** Do not be anxious about anything, but in every situation, by prayer and petition, with thanksgiving, present your requests to God **(Philippians 4:6-7)**

6. **We pray to restore our spiritual lives.** When you pray and ask God to fill you with the knowledge of His will in all spiritual wisdom and understanding, you repair your spiritual life for the better. Prayer enables you to walk in a manner worthy of the Lord, fully pleasing to Him, bearing fruit in every good work and increasing in the knowledge of God **(Colossians 1:9-10).** Pray that you, speaking the truth in love, would grow up in every way into Christ who is the head of the Body, and that He would make the entire Body grow so that it builds itself up in love **(Ephesians 4:16-17).** Ask God to help you be on your guard so that you are not carried away by the error of unprincipled men and fall from your own steadfastness, but would grow in the grace and knowledge of our Lord and Savior Jesus Christ **(2 Peter 3:17-18).**

7. **We pray to reshape into the way God wants us to be.** By praying without ceasing, you gain

knowledge of who God says you are, you can do what he says you can do, and you can become all that he created you to be. Look to the LORD and his strength; seek his face always **(1 Chronicles 16:11).** As children of the almighty God, we want to prevail in spiritual battle. The Bible tells us, "Submit yourselves, then, to God. Resist the devil and he will flee from you" **(James 4:7).** Acknowledge to God almighty that all Scripture is breathed out by Him and profitable for teaching, for reproof, for correction, and for training in righteousness, that you may be competent, equipped for every good work **(2 Timothy 3:16-17).** Ask Him to give you a love for His Word, and a desire to meditate on it all day long **(Psalm 119:97).**

8. **We pray for a balance of emotional, mental, and spiritual wellbeing.** Because God is the source of the strength and stability of our emotional, mental, and spiritual wellness, prayer is one of the most important tools we can use in our quest for a balanced and healthy life. Meditating on the word of God is a mind and body practice that can increase calmness and physical relaxation, improving psychological balance, coping with illness, and enhancing overall health and well-being.

9. I remember the days of long ago; I meditate on all your works and consider what your hands have done **(Psalm 143:5).** I will remember the deeds of the LORD; yes, I will remember your miracles of long ago. I will consider all your works and meditate on all your mighty deeds **(Psalm 77:11-12).** Your commands are always with me and make me wiser than my enemies **(Psalm 119:98).**

10. **We pray because we want to fellowship with God our Heavenly Father.** Through prayer we can communicate with our Heavenly Father and seek His guidance daily. Prayer is a sincere, heartfelt talk with our Heavenly Father. We should pray to God the creator of heaven and earth and not to man- made Gods. We proclaim to you what we have seen and heard, so that you also may have fellowship with us. And our fellowship is with the Father and with his Son, Jesus Christ. **(1 John 1:3).** For anyone who speaks in a tongue does not speak to people but to God. Indeed, no one understands them; they utter mysteries by the Spirit (**1 Corinthians 14:2**).

11. **We Pray to keep our Faith Alive.** We are constantly aware of how much we need God, His grace, His strength, His power working through even the toughest days. We must therefore pray always for Him to help us keep our focus on Him in both good and in bad times. "Simon, Simon, Satan has asked to sift all of you as wheat. But I have prayed for you, Simon, that your faith may not fail. And when you have turned back, strengthen your brothers." **(Luke 22:31-32).** When we pray, we take our burden to God and he helps us keep our faith from fading. As scriptures tells us in **Matthew 11:28**, Jesus says "Come to me all you who labor and are overburdened, and I will give you rest" and in **1 Peter 5:7**, we are admonished to cast all our burdens upon the Lord, for he cares for us.

12. **Prayer is a Platform to make Requests or Petitions.** Prayer is a spiritual tool as important as the oxygen we breath, we simply cannot live without prayers. Through prayer, we express our reverence,

gratitude, and love to God. We make requests or petitions to God. Therefore, I tell you, whatever you ask for in prayer, believe that you have received it, and it will be yours (**Mark 11:24**). Do not be anxious about anything, but in every situation, by prayer and petition, with thanksgiving, present your requests to God (**Philippines 4:6**). When you bring your broken heart and wounds to God in prayer, He heals your brokenheart and binds up your wounds (**Psalm 147:3**).

13. **We pray to acknowledge our total dependency on God.** Prayer is one of the main ways in which we abide. It is how we increase our reliance upon God because we come to understand that without Him, we cannot do or be anything. Many are the plans in a person's heart, but it is the LORD's purpose that prevails (**Proverbs 19:21**). Through prayer, we acknowledge that God is all knowing (omniscience), all present (omnipresent), and all powerful (omnipotent). Omnipotence means that God is in total control of himself and his creation. His omnipresence is a presence both in place and in time. Psalm 139 indicates that God is present in every place. He is the creator of the heavens and the earth, and so he is in every location. This acknowledged dependence causes us to run to God in prayer for everything and anything.

"We do not want you to be uninformed, brothers and sisters, about the troubles we experienced in the province of Asia. We were under great pressure, far beyond our ability to endure, so that we despaired of life itself. Indeed, we felt we had received the sentence of death. But this happened that we might not rely on ourselves but on God, who raises the dead. He has delivered us from such a deadly peril, and he will deliver us again. On him we have set our hope that he will continue to deliver us, as you help us by your prayers. Then many will give thanks on our behalf for the gracious favor granted us in answer to the prayers of man." **(2 Corinthians 1:8-11).**

*Chapter Three*

# WHAT IS A GODLY PRAYER?

**TO BETTER UNDERSTAND** a Godly prayer, let us start by understanding the meaning of prayer. What is prayer? Jesus' disciples in the bible book of Luke 11:1 asked Him to teach them how to pray. Jesus starts His instruction by this, then, is how you should pray:

> *"Our Father in heaven, hallowed be your name, your kingdom come, your will be done, on earth as it is in heaven. Give us today our daily bread. And forgive us our debts, as we also have forgiven our debtors. And lead us not into temptation but deliver us from the evil one." (Mathew 6:9-13)*

Jesus taught this classic lesson in prayer to His disciples. The Lord's Prayer, also called the Model Prayer and the "Our Father," is Jesus' own pattern for how we should approach the Almighty. The Lord's Prayer (Matthew 6:9-13) is Christ's response to the question of how to pray a Godly prayer. The Lord's prayer is one that every Christian should hide in their heart. It is perhaps the most popular prayer in all of Christianity. It is known in many languages and is recited around the world. It teaches us how to relate to God, shows us how to pray and what to pray for. It is notable for its brevity (clear and conciseness), simplicity, and comprehensiveness. Of the 7 petitions, 3 are directed to God and 4 are directed toward human needs. The Lord's prayer contains three main elements: *praise, petition, and a yearning for the coming kingdom of God*. It consists of an introductory address and seven petitions.

After the initial address to the Father, the prayer itself is composed of seven petitions. There are three "thy-petitions" (*thy name, thy kingdom, thy will*) followed by four "us-petitions" (*give us, forgive us, lead us not and deliver us*). In between these petitions is a special petition of forgiveness (*As we forgive others*). To better understand the Lord's Prayer, it is important to briefly examine each petition.

**Thy Name:** There are various names of God, many of which enumerate the various qualities of a Supreme Being. The great purpose of man, especially the believer in Christ, is to glorify God. Essential to our ability to glorify God is the knowledge of God through his various qualities as depicted in his myriad of names. Examples of some names of God include: The Light, King of Kings, Lord of Lords, Lord of Hosts, Ancient of Days, Deliverer, Protector, Exonerator, Comforter, Father/Abba, Most High, Elohim, El-Shaddai, Yahweh, Jehovah, Jehovah Jireh, and Adonai.

**Thy Kingdom:** The Kingdom of God is the realm where God reigns supreme, and Jesus Christ is King. In this kingdom, God's authority is recognized, and his will is obeyed. The concept of a Kingdom of God is not primarily one of space, territory, or politics, as in a national kingdom, but rather one of kingly rule, reign, and sovereign control.

**Thy Will:** The will of God is God's divine plan for humanity. For I know the plans I have for you," declares the LORD, "plans to prosper you and not to harm you, plans to give you hope and a future *(Jeremiah 29:11)*

**Give Us:** God is our Provider. One of the names of God is Jehovah Jireh, which means "the Lord our provider" or "the Lord will provide." It is so wonderful to know that God is our source for everything we need, there is no need so small that He does not know about and nothing too big that He cannot provide for his children.

**Forgive Us:** God is our Exonerator, the forgiver of all sins no matter how big or how small. He forgives sins of commission and sins of omission. "If we confess our sins, he is faithful and just and will forgive us our sins and purify us from all unrighteousness" *(1 John 1:9)*

**As we also have forgiven our debtors:** If we withhold forgiveness to others, forgiveness will also be withheld from us. **(Mathew 6:12)**

**Lead us Not:** God is the greatest Leader of all. He loves, cares, comforts, provides, forgives, mentors and protects his children "Even though I walk through the darkest valley, I will fear no evil, for you are with me; your rod and your staff, they comfort me". *(Psalm 23:4).*

**Deliver Us:** God is our Deliverer from all that is evil. "The LORD is my rock, my fortress and my deliverer; my God is my rock, in whom I take refuge, my shield and the horn of my salvation, my stronghold" *(Psalm 18:2).*

*Prayer is a petition, a solemn request for help or expression of thanks addressed to God or an object of worship. Prayer is an invocation or act that seeks to activate a rapport with an object of worship through deliberate communication.*

*Chapter Four*
# WHEN YOU PRAY, HOLD GOD IN REMEMBRANCE OF HIS PROMISES

**A GODLY PRAYER** that leads to Godly success must focus on the promises of God and not the problems! Isaiah said, put God in remembrance of his promises **(Isaiah 62:6)**. Keep God on the throne always by holding him in remembrance of what his will for your life is. When you put your problems on the throne, you are going the opposite direction from God! God is never obligated to bring to pass what we say, but he is obligated to bring to pass what he promises! God is not a man that he should lie **(Numbers 23:19)**. God cannot lie **(Titus 1:2).** Let us hold unswervingly to the hope we profess, for he who promised is faithful **(Hebrew 10:23).**

**My Testimony of Holding God in Remembrance of His Promises.** By the time Ryan and Bryan (my twin Sons) were two years old, they started exhibiting signs and symptoms of developmental issues especially with their speech! I did all the required testing and finally they were diagnosed with Autism(a developmental disorder of variable severity that is characterized by difficulty in social interaction and communication and by restricted or repetitive patterns of thought and behavior) and ADHD(Attention-deficit/hyperactivity disorder is a brain disorder marked by an ongoing pattern of inattention and/or hyperactivity-impulsivity that interferes with functioning or development)!

When I got the diagnosis of Autism, ADHD, amongst other diagnosis for both of my sons, my world for a moment came crashing! I quickly realized who I was, whose I was and took **Psalm 50:15** to the Lord my God! I went to him unwaveringly day in day out and called unto him to rescue my boys from Autism and other health issues! I promised to glorify him for the rest of my life. I went to him with humility and thanksgiving and sort him like never with all my heart and found him **(Jeremiah 29:13)**.

About eight years after their initial Autism diagnosis, they were completely healed from Autism, ADHD and all the other related diagnosis! Ryan and Bryan are not only very healthy but are well behaved, loving, grateful, kind and the best teenagers any parent could ever ask God for. I have been giving God the Glory ever since and will continue until my mission on this earth is accomplished.

Call unto God in your day of distress, he will rescue you and you will glorify him (**Psalm 50:15**). When you face difficulties, the best way to go about it is to find a promise of God in the Bible and humbly take it to him in prayer and thanksgiving. When you pray, backup every complain with a promise of God! "Father, my world is falling apart, I am in so much distress, but you said if I call on you in my day of distress you will rescue me and I will glorify you." (**Psalm 50:15**).

A GUIDE TO THE PROMISES OF GOD FOR
OUR LIVES, DESTINY AND PURPOSE

1. **God's promises about being with us.** Keep your life free from love of money, and be content with what you have, for God will never leave you nor forsake you **(Hebrews 13:5)**. Neither death nor life, nor angels nor rulers, nor things present nor things to come, nor powers, nor height nor depth, nor anything else in all creation, will be able to separate you from the love of God in Christ Jesus our Lord **(Romans 8:38-39)**. The Lord God has commanded you to be strong and courageous, not to be afraid, not to be discouraged, for He will be with you wherever you go **(Joshua 1:9).** So do not fear, for God is with you; do not be dismayed, for he is your God. He will strengthen you and help you; He will uphold you with his righteous right hand **(Isaiah 41:10).** Be strong and courageous. Do not be afraid or terrified because of them, for the LORD your God goes with you; he will never leave you nor forsake you **(Deuteronomy 31:6).** The LORD your God is with you, the Mighty Warrior who saves. He will take great delight in you; in his love he will no longer rebuke you but will rejoice over you with singing **(Zephaniah 3:17).** The LORD is good to all; he has compassion on all he has made **(Psalm 145:9).** The LORD is near to all who call on him, to all who call on him in truth **(Psalm 145:18).** Even though you walk through the darkest valley, fear no evil, for God is with you; His rod and His staff, they comfort you **(Psalm 23:4).** And teaching them to obey everything I have commanded

you. And surely, I am with you always, to the very end of the age (**Mathew 28:20**).
2. **God's promises to build our faith.** Now faith is confidence in what we hope for and assurance about what we do not see (**Hebrew 11:1**). In all you do, you need faith to move God and climb the ladder to Godly success. You will seek God and find Him when you seek Him with all your heart (**Jeremiah 29:13**). And without faith it is impossible to please God because anyone who comes to him must believe that he exists and that he rewards those who earnestly seek him (**Hebrews 11:6**). God loves you and He is for you! You can pray by faith and get the results you are looking for—because God wants to meet your needs! Trust in the LORD with all your heart and lean not on your own understanding; in all your ways submit to him, and he will make your paths straight (**Proverbs 3:5-6**). Take delight in the LORD, and he will give you the desires of your heart (**Psalm 37:4**). For he will command his angels concerning you to guard you in all your ways (**Psalm 91:11**). Do not be anxious about anything, but in every situation, by prayer and petition, with thanksgiving, present your requests to God. $^7$And the peace of God, which transcends all understanding, will guard your hearts and your minds in Christ Jesus (**Philippians 4:6-7**).
3. **God's promises about answering prayers.** God has not only commanded us to pray, but also promised us that he will answer our prayers through Jesus. Jesus is the way and the truth and the life. When Jesus spoke again to the people, he said, "I am the light of the world. Whoever follows me will

never walk in darkness but will have the light of life." **(John 8:12)**. Jesus is the resurrection and the life. The one who believes in him will live, even though they die **(John 11:25).** No one comes to the Father except through Him **(John 14:6).** God promises that we can be overcomers through the Holy Spirit when we pray in the Name of Jesus. **John 14** continues Jesus' discussions with His disciples in anticipation of His death and records the promised gift of the Holy Spirit **(John 14:15-16).** And If any of us lacks wisdom, we should ask God, who gives generously to all without finding fault, and it will be given to us **(James 1:5).** And when you stand praying, if you hold anything against anyone, forgive them, so that your Father in heaven may forgive you your sins **(Mark 11:25).** In all you do, take delight in the LORD, and he will give you the desires of your heart **(Psalm 37:4)**. Ask and it will be given to you; seek and you will find; knock and the door will be opened to you. For everyone who asks receives; the one who seeks finds; and to the one who knocks, the door will be opened**(Luke 11:9-13)** Then you will call on God and come and pray to Him, and He will listen to you **(Jeremiah 29:12).** God will respond to the prayer of the destitute; he will not despise their plea **(Psalm 102:17).**

4. **God's promises about provision.** God may provide differently than we expect according to His will for our lives. The provisions of God for his people are a common theme throughout scripture. From land, food, and shelter to a righteous path of salvation, God provides for those who follow His commandments. **Philippians 4:19** reminds us

that God will supply all our needs according to His riches in glory in Christ Jesus. So do not worry, saying, 'What shall we eat?' or 'What shall we drink?' or 'What shall we wear?' For the pagans run after all these things, and your heavenly Father knows that you need them. But seek first his kingdom and his righteousness, and all these things will be given to you as well (**Mathew 6:31-33**). God invites all those who are weary and burdened to come to him for him to give them rest (**Mathew 11:28**). Trust in the LORD with all your heart and lean not on your own understanding; in all your ways submit to him, and he will make your paths straight (**Proverbs 3:5-6**). And God is able to bless you abundantly, so that in all things at all times, having all that you need, you will abound in every good work (**2 Corinthians 9:8**). The lions may grow weak and hungry, but those who seek the LORD lack no good thing (**Psalm 34:10**). He who did not spare his own Son, but gave him up for us all-how will he not also, along with him, graciously give us all things? (**Romans 8:32**), The thief comes only to steal and kill and destroy; but Jesus came so that we may have life and have it to the full (**John 10:10**).

5. **God's promises about marriage.** But God's promise for your marriage is that you will be unified emotionally, spiritually, and physically. "However, each one of you also must love his wife as he loves himself, and the wife must respect her husband." (**Ephesians 5:33**). Therefore, what God has joined together, let no one separate (**Mark 10:9**). One of the greatest joys of marriage is the feeling of complete intimacy. Be completely humble and gentle;

be patient, bearing with one another in love. Make every effort to keep the unity of the Spirit through the bond of peace **(Ephesians 4:2-3)**. God reminds us that the head of every man is Christ, and the head of the woman is man, and the head of Christ is God **(1 Corinthians 11:3)**. Be kind and compassionate to one another, forgiving each other, just as in Christ God forgave you **(Ephesians 4:32)**. Submit to one another out of reverence for Christ **(Ephesians 5:21)**. Marriage should be honored by all, and the marriage bed kept pure, for God will judge the adulterer and all the sexually immoral **(Hebrews 13:4)**. Finally, all of you, be like-minded, be sympathetic, love one another, be compassionate and humble. Do not repay evil with evil or insult with insult. On the contrary, repay evil with blessing, because to this you were called so that you may inherit a blessing **(1 Peter 3:8-9)**.

6. **God's Promises about Children.** Children obey your parents in the LORD, for this is right. "Honor your father and mother"-which is the first commandment with a promise- so that it may go well with you and that you may enjoy long life on the earth." Fathers do not exasperate your children; instead, bring them up in the training and instruction of the LORD **(Ephesians 6:1-4)**. Children obey your parents in everything, for this pleases the LORD **(Colossians 3:20)**. Promises for children: my children will rise and call me blessed. My children will be mighty in the land. Children are a blessing from God to be enjoyed! Start children off on the way they should go, and even when they are old, they will not turn from it **(Proverbs 22:6)**. All

your children will be taught by the LORD, and great will be their peace **(Isaiah 54:13).** Be sure of this: The wicked will not go unpunished, but those who are righteous will go free **(Proverbs 11:21).** Praise the LORD. Blessed are those who fear the LORD, who find great delight in his commands. Their children will be mighty in the land; the generation of the upright will be blessed. **(Psalm 112:1-2).** The LORD is good to all; he has compassion on all he has made **(Psalm 145:9).** For I will pour water on the thirsty land, and streams on the dry ground; I will pour out my Spirit on your offspring, and my blessing on your descendants **(Isaiah 44:3).**

7. **God's promises about prosperity.** Biblical blessing is primarily focused on the relationship one has with God. Principally, a person who is blessed is one who is the recipient of God's protection, God's holy pleasure, and God's grace **(Genesis 12:2-3)**. God's Promises for open doors: you promised you will open doors that no one can shut. For I know the plans I have for you," declares the LORD, "plans to prosper you and not to harm you, plans to give you hope and a future **(Jeremiah 29:11).** Do not conform to the pattern of this world but be transformed by the renewing of your mind. Then you will be able to test and approve what God's will is-his good, pleasing, and perfect will **(Romans 12:2)** The house of the wicked will be destroyed, but the tent of the upright will flourish **(Proverbs 14:11).** Be strong and very courageous. Be careful to obey all the law my servant Moses gave you; do not turn from it to the right or to the left, that you may be successful wherever you go. Keep this

Book of the Law always on your lips; meditate on it day and night, so that you may be careful to do everything written in it. Then you will be prosperous and successful **(Joshua 1:7-8).** And observe what the LORD your God requires: Walk in obedience to him, and keep his decrees and commands, his laws, and regulations, as written in the Law of Moses. Do this so that you may prosper in all you do and wherever you go ⁴and that the LORD may keep his promise to me: 'If your descendants watch how they live, and if they walk faithfully before me with all their heart and soul, you will never fail to have a successor on the throne of Israel.' **(1 Kings 2:3-4).** The LORD will send a blessing on your barns and on everything you put your hand to. The LORD your God will bless you in the land he is giving you **(Deuteronomy 28:8).** Those who work their land will have abundant food, but those who chase fantasies have no sense **(Proverbs 12:11).** The greedy stir up conflict, but those who trust in the LORD will prosper **(Proverbs 28:25).**

8. **God's Promises about our health**. God promises good health to all those who follow him diligently. God is more focused on our spiritual health than our physical health. Spiritual health means that we are alive and vibrant in Christ. This promise does not necessarily mean that those who do not follow God will always be sick. Nor does it mean that God's people will be free of disease. The Bible says, "I pray that you may enjoy good health and that all may go well with you, even as your soul is getting along well" **(3 John 1:2).** God gives strength to the weary and increases the power of the weak **(Isaiah**

**40:29).** But those who hope in the LORD will renew their strength. They will soar on wings like eagles; they will run and not grow weary; they will walk and not be faint **(Isaiah 40:31).** For physical training is of some value, but godliness has value for all things, holding promise for both the present life and the life to come **(1 Timothy 4:8).**

9. **God's Promises about our Enemies.** God has promised to deal with our enemies the best way he knows how to. The LORD will grant that the enemies who revolt against you will be defeated before you. They will come at you from one direction but flee from you in seven **(Deuteronomy 28:7).**

10. But to you who are listening I say: Love your enemies, do good to those who hate you, bless those who curse you, pray for those who mistreat you. If someone slaps you on one cheek, turn to them the other also. If someone takes your coat, do not withhold your shirt from them. Give to everyone who asks you, and if anyone takes what belongs to you, do not demand it back. Do to others as you would have them do to you. "If you love those who love you, what credit is that to you? Even sinners love those who love them. And if you do good to those who are good to you, what credit is that to you? Even sinners do that. And if you lend to those from whom you expect repayment, what credit is that to you? Even sinners lend to sinners, expecting to be repaid in full. But love your enemies, do good to them, and lend to them without expecting to get anything back. Then your reward will be great, and you will be children of the Most High, because he is kind to the ungrateful and wicked. Be merciful, just

as your Father is merciful **(Luke 6:27-36)**.
11. Do not take revenge, my dear friends, but leave room for God's wrath, for it is written: "It is mine to avenge; I will repay," says the LORD **(Romans 12:19)**. No weapon forged against you will prevail, and you will refute every tongue that accuses you. This is the heritage of the servants of the LORD, and this is their vindication from me," declares the LORD **(Isaiah 54:17)**. God will prepare a table before you in the presence of your enemies. He will anoint your head with oil; your cup will overflow **(Psalm 23:5)**. For our struggle is not against flesh and blood, but against the rulers, against the authorities, against the powers of this dark world and against the spiritual forces of evil in the heavenly realms. Therefore, put on the full armor of God, so that when the day of evil comes, you may be able to stand your ground, and after you have done everything, to stand **(Ephesians 6:12-13)**.
12. **God's promises about salvation.** God's promises about salvation generally refers to the saving of the soul from sin and its consequences through Christ Jesus. If you confess with your mouth the Lord Jesus and believe in your heart that God has raised Him from the dead, you will be saved **(Romans 10:9)**. For God so loved the world that he gave his one and only Son, that whoever believes in him shall not perish but have eternal life **(John 3:16)**. So, if the Son sets you free, you will be free indeed **(John 8:36)**. If we confess our sins, he is faithful and just and will forgive us our sins and purify us from all unrighteousness **(1 John 1:9 2)**.

*Chapter Five*

# THE PROMISE OF THE HOLY SPIRIT BY JESUS CHRIST

**SPIRIT IS FROM** the Hebrew word *ruah* and Greek *pneuma* which mean breath. Without breath, you cannot be alive. We need the Holy Spirit for renewal and connection with divinity. The Holy Spirit is a special gift promised to us by Jesus while still on earth and delivered on Pentecost. The apostle John records Jesus saying "But the Advocate, the Holy Spirit, whom the Father will send in My name, will teach you all things and will remind you of everything I have told you." **(John 14:26)**. Jesus continues by declaring that "when the advocate comes, whom I will send to you from the Father--the Spirit of truth who goes out from the Father--He will testify about Me"**(John 15:26).**

Jesus advises us all through his disciples to "Pray in the spirit on all occasions with all kinds of prayers and requests" **(John 16:7).** Jesus Christ sent us the holy spirit so that in him we could live, we could move and have our being **(Act 17:28).** We are also warned to be alert and always keep on praying for all the saints **(Ephesians 6:18).**

After the death of Jesus, the Holy Spirit played an important role in the prayer life of the disciples of Christ. Today, the Holy Spirit is crucial in the prayer lives of all believers in Christ Jesus.

The Holy Spirit did not come to replace Jesus but to help us know Jesus better. God's love has been poured into our heart through the workings of the Holy Spirit **(Romans 5:5)**. The Holy Spirit enables us to love God and express unconditional love to others. God never intended that we should be left to pray on our own. So, He gave the Holy Spirit to instruct, inspire, and illumine our hearts and minds. Without the Holy Spirt, we cannot accept Jesus into our lives. He is the one who enables us to cry Abba Father **(Romans 8:15-16).** The Holy Spirit helps in our weakness; teaches us how to pray; makes us fitting temples for God (Holy), strengthens and empowers us to bear witness to Christ.

**The Nine Gifts of the Holy Spirit**. The gifts of the Holy Spirit are internal workings from our relationship with the Holy Spirit. Those who relate with the Holy Spirit will have these gifts. These gifts are Wisdom, Understanding, Knowledge, Faith, Speaking in Tongues, Healing, Prophecy, Interpretation of Tongues, Spiritual Discernment, Miraculous Powers **(1 Corinthians 12:7-11)**

**The Nine Fruits of the Holy Spirit.** The fruits of the Holy Spirit (External Manifestation) are the languages spoken by those filled with the Holy Spirit. The traditional fruits of the Holy Spirit are love, joy, peace, forbearance, kindness, goodness, faithfulness, gentleness, and self-control **(Galatians 5:22-23)**. These gifts are given by the Holy Spirit to individuals to use to bear fruits, but their purpose is to build up the entire Church. They are described in the New Testament, primarily in Romans 12, 1 Corinthians 12:1-3, and Ephesians 4. 1 Peter 4 also touches on the spiritual gifts.

Now about the gifts of the Spirit, brothers, and sisters, I do not want you to be uninformed. You know that when you were pagans, somehow or other you were influenced and led astray to mute idols. Therefore I want you to know that no one who is speaking by the Spirit of God says, "Jesus be cursed," and no one can say, "Jesus is Lord," except by the Holy Spirit **(1 Corinthians 12:1-3).**

**The Invitation of the Holy Spirit During Prayers.** When you pray, always remember to invite, and welcome the holy spirit into your private space by opening the door of your heart and receiving his mighty presence. Surrender yourself to his peace, calmness, fire and let his presence overwhelm and transform you. You can invite him thus *"Come Holy Spirit, fill my heart with your presence, rekindle in me the fire of gratitude, love, joy, peace, forbearance, kindness, goodness, faithfulness, gentleness, and self-control"*

**The Holy Spirit as An Advocate.** An advocate is someone who fights for something or someone, especially someone who fights for the rights of others. An advocate is always for you, never against you! The Holy Spirit is also our Advocate because he can refute the evils, ignorance, and misunderstandings that other people may have about us, and about God. The Holy Spirit is our Advocate, because the Holy Spirit inspires, instructs, and illuminate our souls at its deepest levels.

The Holy Spirit is the Love of God poured into our hearts (Romans 5:5) and drives out unlovely companions of our soul. The Holy Spirit is all of the following and more: Instructor, Inspirator, Illuminator, Champion, Upholder, Supporter, Backer, Promoter, Proponent,

Exponent, Protector, Patron, Spokesperson For, Speaker For, Campaigner For, Fighter For, Battler For, Crusader For, Missionary, Reformer, Pioneer, Pleader, Propagandist, Apostle, Apologist, Booster!

**KEY POINTS ABOUT THE HOLY SPIRIT**

1. The Holy Spirit is the divine power of God Zechariah 4:6; Micah 3:8, 2 Timothy 1:7, Acts 1:8, Romans 15:13, Romans 15:19
2. The Holy Spirit Prophesied the coming of Christ
3. Jesus Christ began His ministry "in the power of the Spirit." Luke 1:35, Acts 10:38, Luke 4:14
4. The work of conviction in the life of an unsaved person is done by the Holy Spirit. (John16:8-9, Acts 2:1-4)
5. God inspires and guides His prophets and servants to reveal his plan through the power of the Holy Spirit. Peter noted that "prophecy never came by the will of man, but holy men of God spoke as they were moved by the Holy Spirit" (2 Peter 1:21). (Ephesians 3:5
6. The Holy Spirit is not only the Spirit of God the Father; it is also "the Spirit of Christ" (Romans 8:9; Philippians 1:19; 1 Peter 1:11). It dwells within Christians, leading and enabling us to be children of God (Romans 8:14).

**WHAT THE BIBLE SAYS ABOUT THE GIFTS OF THE HOLY SPIRIT**

- John 14:26: But the Advocate, the Holy Spirit, whom the Father will send in my name, will teach

you all things and will remind you of everything I have said to you.
- John 15:26: When the Advocate comes, whom I will send to you from the Father-the Spirit of truth who goes out from the Father-he will testify about me.
- John 16:7: But very truly I tell you, it is for your good that I am going away. Unless I go away, the Advocate will not come to you; but if I go, I will send him to you.
- 1 Corinthians 12:7-11: Now to each one the manifestation of the Spirit is given for the common good. To one there is given through the Spirit a message of wisdom, to another a message of knowledge by means of the same Spirit, to another faith by the same Spirit, to another gifts of healing by that one Spirit, to another miraculous powers, to another prophecy, to another distinguishing between spirits, to another speaking in different kinds of tongues, and to still another the interpretation of tongues. All these are the work of one and the same Spirit, and he distributes them to each one, just as he determines.
- Romans 5:5: And hope does not put us to shame, because God's love has been poured out into our hearts through the Holy Spirit, who has been given to us.
- Romans 8:15-16: The Spirit you received does not make you slaves, so that you live in fear again; rather, the Spirit you received brought about your adoption to sonship. And by him we cry, "Abba, Father." The Spirit himself testifies with our spirit that we are God's children.
- Romans 8:23: Not only so, but we ourselves, who

have the first fruits of the Spirit, groan inwardly as we wait eagerly for our adoption to sonship, the redemption of our bodies.
- Ephesians 4:3: Make every effort to keep the unity of the Spirit through the bond of peace.
- Galatians 5:22-23: But the fruit of the Spirit is love, joy, peace, forbearance, kindness, goodness, faithfulness, gentleness, and self-control. Against such things there is no law.

*Chapter Six*

# PRAYING IN AN UNKNOWN TONGUE

**I WAS BORN** and raised as a Catholic Christian and until I was about 13 years old, I knew nothing about praying or speaking in tongues. My first encounter with someone speaking in tongues was at my all girls boarding secondary school in the late 80s. It was a frightening experience and for a while some of us thought she was possessed, and some thought it was an advanced stage of cerebral Malaria! Sooner than later, the rumors about the girl who was speaking in tongues were laid to rest and my ignorance about speaking in an unknown tongue was partially taken care of!

However, my curiosity never pushed me then to try to know more about speaking in tongues except the fact that praying in tongues is real and is a gift of the Holy Spirit!

I was more comfortable then speaking a language I could also understand at least!

I never spoke in an unknown tongue until my early

30s after an encounter with God at the famous Lakeland Florida Revival!

(*The Lakeland Revival, or Florida Healing Outpouring, was an evangelical Christian revival which took place from April until October of 2008 in Lakeland, Florida, United States. The revival began on April 2, 2008, when evangelist Todd Bentley of Fresh Fire Ministries Canada was invited by Stephen Strader, pastor of Lakeland's Ignited Church, to lead a one-week revival, but remained there for over four) months)*

My sister came from Washington DC and drove me to the revival and by then I was on a lot of medications for severe depression, insomnia, and anxiety. We camped out of the revival grounds for five hours before the doors opened! When we got to the entrance, the men ushering people in looked at my sister and I twice and ushered us to the left while most people were ushered to the right! I asked why left side and the unanimous answer was, the left side is for ministers of God! My Sister and I looked at each other and accepted our faith without asking any more questions!

As we mingled and had fellowship with the great men and women of God from all over the world, one of the Ministers moved closer to me and asked me two questions:

Question #1: Do you speak in tongues?

Question # 2: Have you ever asked God to heal your face of severe acne outbreaks?

When I told her in response to the first question that I have not yet leaned how to speak in tongues, she held both of my hands, looked into my eyes and calmly said » you don't have to learn how to pray in tongues, it is a gift from God, pray and ask him to give you the gift of speaking in an unknown tongue »

For the second question I told her I never thought I could pray about my face and acne outbreaks! Again, she looked into my eyes and said, "you can and should pray about anything no matter how big or small and God will heal you."

I thanked her from the bottom of my heart, and we all joined the praise and worship team praising and worshipping God for hours before the speakers started speaking and performing healing miracles I never could imagine before! I witnessed great manifestations of the work of the Holy Spirit—speaking in tongues, ecstatic prophecies, miraculous healings and even the claim that people were being raised from the dead. It was an unimaginable and intriguing experience for me! I felt like a completely new being! Just about every major media outlet in America covered this great revival at one time or another.

At the end of that night, I was healed from depression, anxiety, insomnia, and severe acne outbreaks. I also received healing and blessings for my children, family, and friends. After praying and asking God that evening to bless me with the gift of speaking in tongues, I received that gift and started speaking and praying in tongues at the revival! God understood the unknown tongue and healed me! I got home that night and tossed all my medications in the trash and gave God all the Glory! My life has never been the same since then!

**WHAT THE BIBLE SAYS ABOUT SPEAKING IN TONGUES**

- **Acts 2:1-4:** When the day of Pentecost came, they were all together in one place. Suddenly a sound like the blowing of a violent wind came from heaven

and filled the whole house where they were sitting. They saw what seemed to be tongues of fire that separated and came to rest on each of them. All of them were filled with the Holy Spirit and began to speak in other tongues as the Spirit enabled them.
- **Acts 19:6:** When Paul placed his hands on them, the Holy Spirit came on them, and they spoke in tongues and prophesied.
- **1 Corinthians 1:5:** For in him you have been enriched in every way-with all kinds of speech and with all knowledge-
- **1 Corinthians 14 :2:** For anyone who speaks in a tongue does not speak to people but to God. Indeed, no one understands them; they utter mysteries by the Spirit.
- **1 Corinthians 12:8-11:** To one there is given through the Spirit a message of wisdom, to another a message of knowledge by means of the same Spirit, to another faith by the same Spirit, to another gifts of healing by that one Spirit, to another miraculous powers, to another prophecy, to another distinguishing between spirits, to another speaking in different kinds of tongues, and to still another the interpretation of tongues. All these are the work of one and the same Spirit, and he distributes them to each one, just as he determines.
- **1 Corinthians 13:1**: If I speak in the tongues of men or of angels, but do not have love, I am only a resounding gong or a clanging cymbal.
- **1 Corinthians 14:23:** So, if the whole church comes together and everyone speaks in tongues, and inquirers or unbelievers come in, will they not say that you are out of your mind?

- **1 Corinthians 14:27-28**: If anyone speaks in a tongue, two-or at the most three-should speak, one at a time, and someone must interpret. If there is no interpreter, the speaker should keep quiet in the church and speak to himself and to God.
- **Galatians 5:22:** But the fruit of the Spirit is love, joy, peace, forbearance, kindness, goodness, faithfulness,
- **Mark 16:17**: And these signs will accompany those who believe: In my name they will drive out demons; they will speak in new tongues.

*Chapter Seven*

# THE SPECIAL ROLE OF FORGIVENESS IN GODLY PRAYERS

**IT IS BENEFICIAL** for us to forgive those who have sinned against us before going to God in prayer to ask for our own sins to be forgiven. The role of forgiveness especially in prayer is not new to any believer who knows about Jesus and the Lord's Prayer. If we withhold forgiveness to others, forgiveness will also be withheld from us (Mathew 6:12). Forgiveness is therefore the key to unlocking God's miracle working power. Lack of forgiveness blocks access to the kingdom and to miracle power, therefore going to God in prayer requires a willingness to forgive swiftly and repeatedly. Therefore, if you are offering your gift at the altar and there remember that your brother has something against you, leave your gift there in front of the altar. First go and be reconciled to your brother; then come and offer your gift (Matthew 5:23-24).

Forgive those that have sinned against you to the point where you feel yourself cleansed of resentment and bitterness and are praying for them. If you do not, the lack of forgiveness will make it impossible for God to forgive you. Every prayer request is depended on your relationship to God the Father through God the son and the holy spirit. This relationship is built on the strength of your recognition of Jesus as Lord and Savior, acceptance of the holy spirit as your advocate and your ability to forgive others.

Forgiveness should therefore not be treated as an occasional act, but a constant attitude. Cultivating and maintaining an attitude of forgiveness always is greatly beneficial spiritually, mentally, and emotionally. All of us need forgiveness of sin since we were all born with a sin problem, forgiving others is a prerequisite for our own forgiveness. Lack of forgiveness breaks our fellowship with God. For if you forgive men when they sin against you, your heavenly Father will also forgive you. But if you do not forgive men their sins, your Father will not forgive your sins (Matthew 6:14-15).

It is important that we understand the mind of God through His word. We serve a merciful father who loves us unconditionally. When we know the mind of God concerning His love towards us, it boosts our faith and confidence in forgiving others and asking for his forgiveness. When we forgive ourselves and others, we do not in any way change the past - but we sure do change the future.

**Forgive yourself:** Forgiveness is a gift you give yourself that keeps giving! People must forgive all who need forgiveness. If the first person to forgive is yourself, you need to say, "God, before You, I forgive myself. Whatever I have done, I accept Your forgiveness, and I forgive me." That is a remarkably simple but profound statement, because if we feel that we are under condemnation, we will never have faith to see miracles. "If our heart does not condemn us," the Bible says, "we have confidence toward

God" (1 John 3:21). Forgive yourself to secure your future! As brilliantly stated by the Luminary Dr. Myles Munroe, you are not free until your past has no effect on your future

**Forgive Others:** Forgiveness towards others opens the door to receive forgiveness from God. We must forgive others because of the example of forgiveness that God has given us in Christ (Matthew 18:21-35). Unconditional forgiveness is an affront against justice and a denial of the significance of sin and its cruel effects. Undeserved forgiveness is an expression of divine love and the only basis of our hope for salvation. As Confucius (Confucius was a Chinese philosopher and politician of the Spring and Autumn period who Lived: 551 BC - 479 BC) once said, " those who cannot forgive others break the bridge over which they themselves must pass." Forgiveness is not an option but a necessity for healing and wellbeing.

## WHAT THE BIBLE SAYS ABOUT FORGIVENESS

- **Colossians 3:13:** Bear with each other and forgive one another if any of you has a grievance against someone. Forgive as the LORD forgave you.
- **Ephesians 4:32**: Be kind and compassionate to one another, forgiving each other, just as in Christ God forgave you.
- **Luke 6:35-36**: But love your enemies, do good to them, and lend to them without expecting to get anything back. Then your reward will be great, and you will be children of the Most High, because he is kind to the ungrateful and wicked. [36]Be merciful, just as your Father is merciful.
- **Luke 6:37**: "Do not judge, and you will not be judged. Do not condemn, and you will not be

condemned. Forgive, and you will be forgiven.
- **Mathew 6:12**: And forgive us our debts, as we also have forgiven our debtors.
- **I John 1:9:** If we confess our sins, he is faithful and just and will forgive us our sins and purify us from all unrighteousness.

## What Others Say about Forgiveness

- **Cherie Carter-Scott**: Anger makes you smaller, while forgiveness forces you to grow beyond what you were *(Cherie Carter-Scott (2010). "If Love Is A Game, These Are The Rules", p.94, Random House)*
- **Corrie Ten Boom:** Forgiveness is the key that unlocks the door of resentment and the handcuffs of hatred. It is a power that breaks the chains of bitterness and the shackles of selfishness *(Corrie Ten Boom (1985). "Jesus is Victor", Fleming H Revell Company)*
- **Mother Teresa**: Whatever our religion, we know that if we really want to love, we must first learn to forgive before anything else *(Mother Teresa (1997). "No Greater love")*
- **Mahatma Gandhi**: The weak can never forgive. Forgiveness is the attribute of the strong. *(Mahatma Gandhi (2005). "All Men Are Brothers", p.166, A&C Black)*
- **Marianne Williamson:** Forgiveness is not always easy. At times, it feels more painful than the wound we suffered, to forgive the one that inflicted it. And yet, there is no peace without forgiveness *(Marianne Williamson (2013). "Illuminata: Thoughts, Prayers, Rites of Passage", p.131, Random House)*
- **Stormie Omartian**: Forgiveness does not make

the other person right; it makes you free (*Stormie Omartian (2010). "Seven Prayers That Will Change Your Life Forever", p.47, Thomas Nelson Inc*
- **Voltaire**: We are all full of weakness and errors; let us mutually pardon each other our follies - it is the first law of nature (*Voltaire (1824). "A Philosophical Dictionary: From the French", p.272)*

*Chapter Eight*

# THE CRUCIAL ROLE OF GRATITUDE IN GODLY PRAYERS

**THE WORD GRATITUDE** is from the Latin root "gratus," meaning "pleasing, agreeable, thankful". Gratitude is the quality of being thankful, readiness to show appreciation for and to return kindness. Praying to God with an attitude of gratitude always is one of the most effective ways of experiencing the power of the holy spirit in touch with your soul. And when the holy spirit connects you with your soul, you can eavesdrop on the wisdom of the creator of the universe. This divine connection enables you to embrace the wisdom of uncertainty and privy to infinite possibilities of divine knowledge and understanding. When you appreciate all Jehovah God has already done in your life, that attitude of gratitude will enable you to see God's concern into everything that concerns you, and be at peace knowing he, the almighty will do again and again what he did for you in the past.

An attitude of gratitude will fuel your measure of faith and make you experience the mighty power of God.

When you are experiencing gratitude, your ego moves out of the way because gratitude and ego cannot coexist! An attitude of gratitude will enable you to encourage yourself into victory, strength, and favor. Hence it becomes easier for Jehovah God to accompany your vision with provision according to the riches of his glory in Christ Jesus (**Philippians 4:19**).

    **G**ratefulness, feeling or showing an appreciation of kindness; thankful.

    **R**ecognition, acknowledgment of something's existence, validity, or legality.

    **A**ppreciativeness, feeling or showing gratitude or pleasure.

    **T**hankfulness, expressing gratitude and relief

    **I**ndebtedness, the feeling of owing gratitude for a service or favor.

    **T**eachability, Able and grateful to learn God's Love and insights by being taught

    **U**nderstanding, having insight or good judgment.

    **D**evotedness, a state of being faithful

    **E**nthusiasm, intense and eager enjoyment, interest, or approval.

Gratitude as a virtue is very significant in facilitating other virtues like Chastity, Charity, Diligence, Faith, Fortitude, Humility, Justice, Patience, Prudence, Temperance, and must be given the attention that it deserves. When gratitude is added as an ingredient to other virtues, it can increasingly benefit the soul and channel it to hunger and thirst for righteousness. Give thanks to God for everything, in all circumstances, for his love, righteousness, mercy and goodness endures forever.

- **Ephesians 5:20:** Always giving thanks to God the Father for Everything, in the name of our LORD Jesus Christ.
- **Mathew 11:25:** At that time Jesus said, "I praise you, Father, LORD of heaven and earth, because you have hidden these things from the wise and learned and revealed them to little children.
- **1 Thessalonians 5:18:** Give thanks in all Circumstances; for this is God's will for you in Christ Jesus.
- **Psalm 7:17:** I will give thanks to the LORD because of his Righteousness; I will sing the praises of the name of the LORD Most High.
- **1 Chronicles 16:34:** Give thanks to the LORD, for he is Good; his Love endures forever.
- **Psalm 25:6:** Remember, LORD, your great Mercy and Love, for they are from of old.
- **Psalm 69:30:** I will praise God's name in song and glorify him with thanksgiving.
- **Psalm 95:2:** Let us come before him with thanksgiving and extol him with music and song.
- **Psalm 100:4:** Enter his gates with thanksgiving and his courts with praise; give thanks to him and praise his name
- **Psalm 136:1-3:** Give thanks to the LORD, for he is good. His love endures forever. Give thanks to the God of gods. His love endures forever. Give thanks to the LORD of lords: His love endures forever.
- **Philippians 4:6-7:** Do not be anxious about anything, but in every situation, by prayer and petition, with thanksgiving, present your requests to God.

And the peace of God, which transcends all understanding, will guard your hearts and your minds in Christ Jesus
- **Hebrews 12:28:** Therefore, since we are receiving a kingdom that cannot be shaken, let us be thankful, and so worship God acceptably with reverence and awe,
- **Colossians 3:17:** And whatever you do, whether in word or deed, do it all in the name of the LORD Jesus, giving thanks to God the Father through him.

*Chapter Nine*

# THE CRUCIAL ROLE OF FASTING IN GODLY PRAYERS

**WHAT IS FASTING?** Fasting is the willful refrainment from eating for a period. Fasting is essentially giving up food or other natural pleasures for a period to focus your thoughts on God. While fasting, many people read the Bible, pray, or worship. Fasting is found throughout the Old and New Testaments of the Bible, over fifty times! It takes your body and submits it to the spirit where the fire of love, joy, peace, longsuffering, kindness, goodness, faithfulness, gentleness, and self-control (**Galatians 5:22-23**) dwell. Fasting increases our spiritual capacity thus enhancing our spiritual consciousness. This means that, when deprived of food for some time, our mind gravitates toward fulfilling needs beyond those of the body. Fasting enhances the solemnity and sacredness of our thoughts and encourages an attitude of piety and God-consciousness. **Joel 2:12** "Yet even now," declares the Lord, "return to me with all your heart, with fasting, with weeping, and with mourning." The desire of God for Israel was that they returned to Him before the Day of the Lord and to do so with "all your heart, with fasting, with weeping, and with mourning."

Fasting restrains our physical pleasure, but it enhances our spiritual pleasure. Our greatest pleasure comes by feasting on the person of Jesus. Fasting reduces the influence of our self-will and invites the Holy Spirit to do more intense work in us. Christian fasting, at its root, is the hunger of a homesickness for God. There are so many benefits and reasons for fasting and so many ways to do it. Find out the best way and how long you plan on fasting as dictated by your reasons for fasting.

Always remember that fasting is strictly a personal thing between you and God and is no one else's business. If you tell people that you are fasting, they might think you are boasting about it or they might think you are acting self-righteously.

**The Impact of Fasting in Prayers.** Fasting is the most powerful force in prayer. Fasting and prayer is one of the most powerful spiritual combinations on earth capable of moving God to move mountains. Spiritual fasting is a way of denying the flesh the basic need for food. While fasting, the physical body is weakened while the spiritual body is strengthened. It is also important to note that fasting is an act of taking the time to seek and listen to the Holy Spirit. True fasting brings humility and alignment with God. It breaks the power of flesh and demons and bad habits. It kills unbelief and brings answers to prayer when nothing else works. Fasting quietens the heart and calms the spirit for a better and fruitful interaction with God and the holy spirit. Fasting brings about a Godly intimacy and keeps God on the throne where he rightly belongs.

Apart from the prayer benefits fasting has also been shown to have many health benefits, from increased weight loss to better brain function. Fasting Promotes Detoxification, Improves Insulin Sensitivity, Rests Digestive System, Boosts Immunity, Corrects High Blood Pressure, promotes weight loss, promote healthy diet etc.

**WHAT THE BIBLE SAYS ABOUT PRAYER AND FASTING.**

- **Acts 13:2-4:** While they were worshiping the LORD and fasting, the Holy Spirit said, "Set apart for me Barnabas and Saul for the work to which I have called them." So, after they had fasted and prayed, they placed their hands on them and sent them off. The two of them, sent on their way by the Holy Spirit, went down to Seleucia and sailed from there to Cyprus.
- **Acts 14:23.** Paul and Barnabas appointed elders for them in each church and, with prayer and fasting, committed them to the LORD, in whom they had put their trust.
- **1 Corinthians 7:5:** Do not deprive each other except perhaps by mutual consent and for a time, so that you may devote yourselves to prayer. Then come together again so that Satan will not tempt you because of your lack of self-control.
- **2 Samuel 1:12:** They mourned and wept and fasted till evening for Saul and his son Jonathan, and for the army of the LORD and for the nation of Israel, because they had fallen by the sword.
- **Matthew 4:1-4:** Jesus answered, "It is written: 'Man shall not live on bread alone, but on every word that comes from the mouth of God.'"
- **Mathew 6:16-18:** When you fast, do not look somber as the hypocrites do, for they disfigure their

faces to show others they are fasting. Truly I tell you, they have received their reward in full. But when you fast, put oil on your head and wash your face, so that it will not be obvious to others that you are fasting, but only to your Father, who is unseen; and your Father, who sees what is done in secret, will reward you.

- **Luke 2:37:** And then was a widow until she was eighty-four. She never left the temple but worshiped night and day, fasting and praying.
- **Luke 4:1-4:** Jesus, full of the Holy Spirit, left the Jordan and was led by the Spirit into the wilderness, where for forty days he was tempted by the devil. He ate nothing during those days, and at the end of them he was hungry. The devil said to him, "If you are the Son of God, tell this stone to become bread." Jesus answered, "It is written: 'Man shall not live on bread alone.'"

*Chapter Ten*

# GOD'S WILL FOR OUR LIVES

**GOD'S WILL FOR** our lives is intertwined in the very word **WILL**! His will for us all is in His Word, Intentions, Love and Legacy! God's Word communicates His Intentions to us! His Intentions reveal his Love for us! His Love guarantees a Heavenly Legacy for us in Christ Jesus. And his Legacy for us is warranted when we seek first his kingdom and his righteousness (Mathew 6:33).

**WHAT IS GOD'S WORD FOR US?**

God's Word communicates His Intentions to us! I believe with every fiber of my being that the Bible is the Word of God because of its scientific accuracy. The Truth of the Word of God tells us that God "hangeth the earth upon nothing" (Job 26:7). All of Scripture is Given to Us by inspiration from God the Father. The Word of God is living and powerful, it is pure, solid truth. The Word of God can sanctify us. God's Word empowers us and enables us to go all the way in our pursuit of Him. God's word says what is true, demands what is right and provides what is good. Our job is to study and apply the Word. It is our weapon against everything that comes against us, whether sickness, fear, or evil thoughts. God's Word is the standard by which we measure our lives and conform to His will.

- What does the Bible say about God's word?

    **John 1:1:** In the beginning was the Word, and the Word was with God, and the Word was God.
    **John 15:7**: If you remain in me and my words remain in you, ask whatever you wish, and it will be done for you.
    **James 1:22:** Do not merely listen to the word, and so deceive yourselves. Do what it says
    **Luke 11:28**: He replied, "Blessed rather are those who hear the word of God and obey it."
    **1 Peter 4:1:** Whoever preaches, let it be with the words of God; whoever serves, let it be with the strength that God supplies, so that in all things God may be glorified through Jesus Christ, to whom belong glory and dominion forever and ever. Amen."
    **Romans 8:26:** In the same way, the Spirit helps us in our weakness. We do not know what we ought to pray for, but the Spirit himself intercedes for us through wordless groans.
    **1 Thessalonians 2:13**: And we also thank God continually because, when you received the word of God, which you heard from us, you accepted it not as a human word, but as it actually is, the word of God, which is indeed at work in you who believe.
    **Proverbs 1:7:** The fear of the Lord is the

beginning of knowledge, but fools despise wisdom and instruction.

**Proverbs 3:7:** Do not be wise in your own eyes; fear the LORD and shun evil.

### WHAT ARE GOD'S INTENTIONS FOR US?

His Intentions as communicated in his word reveal his Love for us. Like a good father, God wants us to be happy. He wants us to dream big and follow our dreams. He wants us to have, nourish and maintain a good relationship with him. God's intentions are to prosper us, give us hope and a future and not to harm us (Jeremiah 29:11). In the Gospel of Matthew, we are told, "It is not the will of your Father which is in heaven, that one of these little ones should perish." (Matthew 18: 14). Knowing God and God's ways helps us to understand that God does not will or wish this suffering on any of us. God's will be not about evil or unpleasantness, disaster, or unhappiness. God intentionally pours out love, mercy, and absolute goodness. This simply leads us to understand that everything that happens is NOT God's will. It is entirely possible for any one of us to work toward the accomplishment of our personal will whether it is in alignment with God. This is the reality of the true freedom given to us by God. We must understand that free will is the most precious but dangerous gift ever given to man! It is God's intention to protect us against all evil and give us strength. It is his plan to not leave nor forsake you! God created us with the intention that we will always live in His presence. We must be connected to Him because it is only in Him that life exists. God is our natural environment. GOD without man is always GOD but man without GOD is nothing!

- What does the Bible say about God's Intentions?

   **Jeremiah 29:11:** For I know the plans I have for you," declares the LORD, "plans to prosper you and not to harm you, plans to give you hope and a future.

   **Jeremiah 33:3:** Call to me and I will answer you and tell you great and unsearchable things you do not know.'

   **Matthew 18: 14:** In the same way your Father in heaven is not willing that any of these little ones should perish.

   **1 Corinthians 10:13**. No temptation has overtaken you except what is common to mankind. And God is faithful; he will not let you be tempted beyond what you can bear. But when you are tempted, he will also provide a way out so that you can endure it.

   **1 John 5:14:** This is the confidence we have in approaching God: that if we ask anything according to his will, he hears us.

   **2 Thessalonians 3:3**. But the LORD is faithful, and he will strengthen you and protect you from the evil one.

   **Deuteronomy** 31:6. Be strong and courageous. Do not be afraid or terrified because of them, for the LORD your God goes with you; he will never leave you nor forsake you."

   **Isaiah 41:10**. So do not fear, for I am with you; do not be dismayed, for I am your God. I will strengthen you and help you; I will uphold you with my righteous right hand.

## How does God display his Love for us?

God's intentions as written in his word reveal his Love for us and His Love guarantees a Heavenly Legacy for us in Christ Jesus. God showed his love for us when he sent his only Son into the world to give us life. And God showed his love for us by sending his only Son into the world, so that we might have life through him. God's love was revealed among us in this way: God sent His One and Only Son into the world so that we might live through Him.

- What does the Bible say about God's Love?

    **John 3:16:** For God so loved the world that he gave his one and only Son, that whoever believes in him shall not perish but have eternal life.
    **1 John 4:7:** Dear friends, let us love one another, for love comes from God. Everyone who loves has been born of God and knows God.
    **1 John 4:8:** Whoever does not love does not know God, because God is love.
    **1 John 4:16:** And so, we know and rely on the love God has for us. God is love. Whoever lives in love lives in God, and God in them.
    **1 John 4:19**: We love because God first loved us
    **Deuteronomy 7:9:** Know therefore that the LORD your God is God; he is the faithful God, keeping his covenant of love to a thousand generations of those who love him and keep his commandments.
    **Ephesians 2:4-5:** But because of his great love for us, God, who is rich in mercy, made us alive with Christ even when we were dead in transgressions-it

is by grace you have been saved.

**1 Peter 5:6-7:** Humble yourselves, therefore, under God's mighty hand, that he may lift you up in due time. Cast all your anxiety on him because he cares for you.

**Psalm 86:15:** But you, LORD, are a compassionate and gracious God, slow to anger, abounding in love and faithfulness.

**Romans 5:8:** But God demonstrates his own love for us in this: While we were still sinners, Christ died for us.

**Romans 8:37-39:** No, in all these things we are more than conquerors through him who loved us. For I am convinced that neither death nor life, neither angels nor demons, neither the present nor the future, nor any powers, neither height nor depth, nor anything else in all creation, will be able to separate us from the love of God that is in Christ Jesus our LORD.

**Zephaniah 3:17:** The LORD your God is with you, the Mighty Warrior who saves. He will take great delight in you; in his love he will no longer rebuke you but will rejoice over you with singing."

### WHAT LEGACY DO WE HAVE IN CHRIST JESUS?

God's Word communicates His Intentions to us! His Intentions reveal his Love for us! His Love guarantees a Heavenly Legacy for us in Christ Jesus. Through faith, we all have a legacy in Christ Jesus as children of God (Galatians 3:26). As believers in Christ Jesus, our legacy should be one of incredible generosity of our time, money, resources, and energy. God started a legacy of giving by sacrificing his only begotten son to come to earth and die for our sins! The benefits of inheritance in Jesus Christ begin for any of us when we accept Jesus as Lord and

Savior. When this is done, something heavenly happens, the Holy Spirit is granted to us as a deposit, a down payment, a promise of the coming eternal life.

- What does the Bible say about our legacy in Christ Jesus?

    **John 14:27:** Peace I leave with you; my peace I give you. I do not give to you as the world gives. Do not let your hearts be troubled and do not be afraid.
    **John 20:29:** Then Jesus told him, "Because you have seen me, you have believed; blessed are those who have not seen and yet have believed."
    **John 20:31:** But these are written that you may believe that Jesus is the Messiah, the Son of God, and that by believing you may have life in his name.
    **Colossians 3:15:** Let the peace of Christ rule in your hearts, since as members of one body you were called to peace. And be thankful.
    **1 Peter 5:10:** And the God of all grace, who called you to his eternal glory in Christ, after you have suffered a little while, will himself restore you and make you strong, firm and steadfast.
    **1 Corinthians 1:8:** He will also keep you firm to the end, so that you will be blameless on the day of our LORD Jesus Christ.
    **2 Corinthians 1:**21: Now it is God who makes both us and you stand firm in Christ. He anointed us,
    **1 Thessalonians 3:13:** May he strengthen your hearts so that you will be blameless and holy in the

presence of our God and Father when our LORD Jesus comes with all his holy ones.

**Philippians 4:7:** And the peace of God, which transcends all understanding, will guard your hearts and your minds in Christ Jesus.

**Romans 5:**1: Therefore, since we have been justified through faith, we have peace with God through our LORD Jesus Christ

**Romans 16:**25: Now to him who is able to establish you in accordance with my gospel, the message I proclaim about Jesus Christ, in keeping with the revelation of the mystery hidden for long ages past,

**Psalm 112:**1: Praise the LORD. Blessed are those who fear the LORD, who find great delight in his commands.

In order for God to fulfil his Word, Intentions, Love and Legacy (WILL) in our lives, we must trust him unconditionally for what we see, what we do not see, what we know, what we do not know, and for what we have heard as well as what we have not heard! We must trust the wisdom and perfection of God's will for our lives by surrendering our will for God 's will. God Desires our willing obedience motivated by love and gratitude! We must trust God's WILL for our lives because he has a plan for us (Jeremiah 29:11).

We must trust God's WILL for our lives because he is our refuge (Psalm 62:6-8). We must trust God's WILL for our lives because he will fight for us (Exodus 14:14). We must trust God's WILL for our lives because He thinks about us (Psalm 139:17). We must trust God's WILL for our lives because He is always with us (Mathew 29:20). We must trust God's WILL for our lives because he knows every single one of us by name (Isaiah 43:1). We must trust God's WILL for our lives because He loved us first before we ever loved him (1 John 4:19).

*Chapter Eleven*

# WHEN YOU PRAY, PRAY ACCORDING TO GOD'S WILL

**GOD'S WILL FOR** us is that we should come to repentance and not perish (2 Peter 3:9). George Mueller (1805-1898) of Bristol, England was one of the mightiest men of prayer in his time and according to him, the safest way to know that you are praying in God's will is to pray God's Word! The ruling motive in our prayers should be that God's will be accomplished, first for ourselves, and second in our prayers for the others.

God's will for our lives is for us to be saved from our sin through prayers and repentance (Repentance is the act of regretting sincerely the sin in your past with the goal to never do it again. It is deciding to turn away from evil and to serve God). God Desires our obedience for his will in our lives motivated by love and gratitude!

We must therefore trust the wisdom and perfection of God's will for our lives by surrendering our will for God 's will. Not everyone who says to me, 'Lord, Lord,' will enter the kingdom of heaven, but only the one who does the will of my Father who is in heaven (Matthew 7:21). Trust in God's will almighty through Christ Jesus because the Christian view of God's will I believe is the only truly consistent, coherent, and rational explanation of God's love and true nature!

Understanding God's will for our lives means acknowledging that though not everyone will be healed, everyone can be saved! And in this process, we have the comfort of knowing that He will never give us more than we can bear. (1 Corinthians 10:13). God's will for our lives consist of His perfect plan known since the beginning of time, His teachings for all people, His specific desires for a community of people, or His unique plan for our individual lives. God's will for our lives is intertwined in in His Word to challenge and empower us to live according to His will. Praying according to God's will enables us to be saved and anchored to a life of victory.

## What the Bible Says about Praying According to God's Will

- **1 John 5:14**: "This is the confidence we have in approaching God: that if we ask anything according to his will, he hears us."
- **Jeremiah 42:3**: "Pray that the LORD your God will tell us where we should go and what we should do."
- **Colossians 1:9:** "For this reason, since the day we heard about you, we have not stopped praying for you. We continually ask God to fill you with the knowledge of his will through all the wisdom and understanding that the Spirit gives,"

- **Mathew 6:9-11:** This, then, is how you should pray: "Our Father in heaven, hallowed be your name, your kingdom come, your will be done, on earth as it is in heaven. Give us today our daily bread."
- **Mathew 21:21-22:** Jesus replied, "Truly I tell you, if you have faith and do not doubt, not only can you do what was done to the fig tree, but also you can say to this mountain, 'Go, throw yourself into the sea,' and it will be done. If you believe, you will receive whatever you ask for in prayer."
- **James 4:3:** "When you ask, you do not receive, because you ask with wrong motives, that you may spend what you get on your pleasures."
- **John 9:31:** "We know that God does not listen to sinners. He listens to the godly person who does his will."
- **Romans 1:10:** "In my prayers at all times; and I pray that now at last by God's will the way may be opened for me to come to you."

## Chapter Twelve
# WHEN WE PRAY, WE MUST PRAISE GOD BY SINGING

**WHEN WE PRAISE** God by singing with an attitude of awe, reverence, and respect, it gives God pleasure! Praise and worship are an essential part of a Godly prayer. We must recognize that God is our Creator, our shield, provider, healer, and our hope for eternal life in Christ Jesus. Praising God shows our gratitude for his goodness, in everything we should give thanks to God.

As the Psalmist says, everything that has breath should praise the Lord (**Psalm 150:6**). Singing to God as a form of praise and worship facilitates access to God. About midnight Paul and Silas were praying and singing hymns to God, and the other prisoners were listening to them. Suddenly there was such a violent earthquake that the foundations of the prison were shaken. At once all the prison doors flew open, and everyone's chains came loose (**Acts 16:25-27**).

The purpose of singing to God, is to praise and worship Him. We praise and worship him for who He is and for all His wonderful works, especially for His grace in accepting us and saving us **(Eph. 1:5-7)**. God invites praise of all kinds from His creation. Praise is so important to God that Jesus said if people do not praise God, even the "stones will cry out" **(Luke 19:40)**. God sees the heart, and He desires and deserves sincere, heartfelt praise and worship. All the earth must sing to the Lord; proclaim his salvation day after day, declare his glory among the nations and his marvelous deeds among all peoples **(1 Chronicles 16:23-24)**.

### What the Bible Says about Praising and Worshiping God

> **Colossians 3:16:** Let the message of Christ dwell among you richly as you teach and admonish one another with all wisdom through psalms, hymns, and songs from the Spirit, singing to God with gratitude in your hearts.
> **1 Corinthians 14:16:** Otherwise when you are praising God in the Spirit, how can someone else, who is now put in the position of an inquirer, say "Amen" to your thanksgiving, since they do not know what you are saying?
> **Ephesians 5:19:** speaking to one another with psalms, hymns, and songs from the Spirit. Sing and make music from your heart to the LORD,
> **Hebrews 13:15:** Through Jesus, therefore, let us continually offer to God a sacrifice of praise-the fruit of lips that openly profess his name.
> **Psalm 150:3-6:** Praise him with the sounding of the trumpet, praise him with the harp and lyre, ⁴praise him with timbrel and dancing, praise him

with the strings and pipe, ⁵praise him with the clash of cymbals, praise him with resounding cymbals. ⁶Let everything that has breath praise the LORD. Praise the LORD.

**Revelations 5:11-12:** Then I looked and heard the voice of many angels, numbering thousands upon thousands, and ten thousand times ten thousand. They encircled the throne and the living creatures and the elders. In a loud voice they were saying: "Worthy is the Lamb, who was slain,

*Chapter Thirteen*
# WE MUST PRAY WITHOUT CEASING

To **"PRAY WITHOUT** ceasing" refers to recurring prayer, not nonstop talking. Prayer is to be a way of life--you are to be continually in an attitude of prayer. It is living in continual God-consciousness, where everything you see and experience becomes a kind of prayer, lived in deep awareness of and surrender to Him. Unceasing prayer is continual dependence upon and communion with the Father. For Christians, prayer should be like breathing.

Praying without ceasing is all about developing a lifestyle of prayer so that you don't just get up in the morning and have a stated time of 10 to 20 minutes of prayer and then you don't pray again until the evening. The heart attitude of praying without ceasing means an ever-open heart to the Lord's leading with a spirit of dependence that should permeate all we do. This is the very spirit and essence of prayer. So, even when we are not speaking consciously to God, there is a deep, abiding dependence on him that is woven into the heart of faith.

Praying without ceasing essentially means that when we commit ourselves to God, we are to submit everything we do to His will. To always be in communion with Him. it means to keep God ever in your thoughts throughout your day, speaking with Him always. Remember Him in all you do and say. We must never forget that prayer was a necessary part of every event in Jesus Christ's life.

### How to Pray without Ceasing

The first step to praying without ceasing is to memorize the Lord's prayer and study what each verse in Mathew 6:9-14 means. Reflect on the meaning so that you can get a spiritually in-depth understanding of the Lord's prayer. Pray without ceasing by waiting on the Lord prayerfully, by staying connected with people of faith, by being active in witnessing to the gospel of God, by being consistent in your prayer, and by seeking strength from the holy spirit.

### What the Bible Says about Praying without Ceasing

> **Colossians 4:2:** Devote yourselves to prayer, being watchful and thankful.
> **1 Thessalonian 5:17-18-:** Pray continually, give thanks in all circumstances; for this is God's will for you in Christ Jesus.
> **Jeremiah 33:3:** Call to me and I will answer you and tell you great and unsearchable things you do not know.
> **John 14:13:** And I will do whatever you ask in my name, so that the Father may be glorified in the Son
> **John 15:7**: If you remain in me and my words remain in you, ask whatever you wish, and it will be

done for you.

**1 Peter 5:7:** Cast all your anxiety on him because he cares for you.

**Philippians 4:6:** Do not be anxious about anything, but in every situation, by prayer and petition, with thanksgiving, present your requests to God.

**Ephesians 6:18:** And pray in the Spirit on all occasions with all kinds of prayers and requests. With this in mind, be alert and always keep on praying for all the LORD's people.

**Psalm 37:4:** Take delight in the LORD, and he will give you the desires of your heart.

**Psalm 162:2:** I will praise the LORD all my life; I will sing praise to my God as long as I live

**Romans 8:26:** In the same way, the Spirit helps us in our weakness. We do not know what we ought to pray for, but the Spirit himself intercedes for us through wordless groans.

**Romans 12:12:** Be joyful in hope, patient in affliction, faithful in prayer.

**2 Chronicles 7:14:** if my people, who are called by my name, will humble themselves and pray and seek my face and turn from their wicked ways, then I will hear from heaven, and I will forgive their sin and will heal their land.

*Chapter Fourteen*

# PATIENCE AS THE GREATEST PRAYER

**PATIENCE IS A** *virtue* and talked about throughout the Bible in the Old and New Testaments. Patience is the capacity to accept or tolerate delay, trouble, or suffering without getting angry or upset. According to 1 Samuel "lack of patience can cause you to miss blessings." Being patient is a vital part of trusting in God as our life circumstances are not always what we would prefer. Patience is a useful skill and a great aspect of one's personality with life enhancing benefits. The holy spirit produces life enhancing fruits in our lives such as love, joy, peace, patience, kindness, goodness, faithfulness, gentleness, and self-control **(Galatians 5:22-23).**

When we take our prayers and supplications to God, the period of waiting for feedback can be a time of fear, intimidation, anxiety, more prayers and supplications, and anchoring on the promises of God! Whatever the waiting attitude, God wants us to be still and trust him! **(Psalm 46:10).** God wants us to have a healthy rest in his presence.

He commands us to wake up, stop striving, and acknowledge him for who He is, allowing Him to do what only He can do.

Waiting on God is good and very productive. Waiting on God requires an uplifted heart! So, wait on God with a grateful heart and a humble spirit! Wait on God prayerfully! Stay connected with people of faith while waiting on God! Seek strength from the holy spirit while waiting on God! Be consistent in your prayer while waiting on God! Be courageous and trust God for the best! Always remember that God's time is the best!

- What the Bible says about Patience

    **Ecclesiastes 7:9**: Do not be quickly provoked in your spirit, for anger resides in the lap of fools.
    **Ephesians 4:2:** Be completely humble and gentle; be patient, bearing with one another in love.
    **Galatians 6:9:** Let us not become weary in doing good, for at the proper time we will reap a harvest if we do not give up.
    **Genesis 29:20:** So, Jacob served seven years to get Rachel, but they seemed like only a few days to him because of his love for her.
    **James 1:2-4:** Consider it pure joy, my brothers, and sisters, whenever you face trials of many kinds, because you know that the testing of your faith produces perseverance. Let perseverance finish its work so that you may be mature and complete, not lacking anything.
    **James 1:3:** Because you know that the testing of your faith produces perseverance.
    **James 1:19**: My dear brothers and sisters, take

note of this: Everyone should be quick to listen, slow to speak and slow to become angry,

**James 5:7-8:** Be patient, then, brothers and sisters, until the LORD's coming. See how the farmer waits for the land to yield its valuable crop, patiently waiting for the autumn and spring rains. You too, be patient and stand firm, because the LORD's coming is near.

**Mathew 7:7:** "Ask and it will be given to you; seek and you will find; knock and the door will be opened to you.

**Psalms 37:7:** Be still before the LORD and wait patiently for him; do not fret when people succeed in their ways, when they carry out their wicked schemes.

**Psalm 46:10:** He says, "Be still, and know that I am God; I will be exalted among the nations, I will be exalted in the earth."

**Proverbs 15:18:** A hot-tempered person stirs up conflict, but the one who is patient calms a quarrel.

**Proverbs 25:15:** Through patience a ruler can be persuaded, and a gentle tongue can break a bone.

**Romans 5:3-4**: Not only so, but we also glory in our sufferings, because we know that suffering produces perseverance; perseverance, character; and character, hope.

**Romans 8:25:** But if we hope for what we do not yet have, we wait for it patiently.

**Romans 12:12:** Be joyful in hope, patient in affliction, faithful in prayer.

*Chapter Fifteen*

# FOURTEEN STEPS TO PRAYING A GODLY PRAYER

**PRAY IN JESUS' Name.** After the birth, life, death, and resurrection of Jesus Christ, praying to God took a turn for the better. Christians now have Jesus Christ directly and permanently plugged to God giving us smooth and unconditional access to God through him. We must therefore go to God through his only begotten son Jesus Christ. When you pray to God through Jesus, always remember to trust, and obey! There is no other way to be happy in Jesus but to trust that he is the son of God, he is for you, and obey his message of love and forgiveness. When we pray in Jesus' name, we unite with Christ according to the will and purpose of God through the Spirit. And God the Father makes certain that His answers to our prayers bring Him glory and honor the Son.

Praying in Jesus' name means that we are conscious of two primary truths as we bring our requests to God: Acknowledgment of His Intercession and Submission to the Will of God. The concept of praying in Jesus' name is biblical. The key text is **John 14:13-14**: "Whatever you ask *in my name*, this I will do, that the Father may be glorified in the Son. If you ask me anything *in my name*, I will do it." Jesus answered, "I am the way and the truth and the life. No one comes to the Father except through me". **Mathew 21:22** adds that if we believe we will receive whatever we ask for in prayer. It is by the name of Jesus Christ of Nazareth, who was crucified but whom God raised from the dead, that we are healed. **(Acts 4:10).**

This concept is repeated a few more times in **John 15:16** and **John 16:23-24**. In these verses, Jesus seems to be saying that prayer given in the name of Jesus is guaranteed to be answered.

**Have Faith**. Now faith is the substance of things hoped for, the evidence of things not seen (Hebrew 11:1). Our faith activates God's infinite grace and makes what is already real in the spiritual realm become manifest in the physical realm. God's will must be accomplished on earth through His submitted servants' faith in the risen Lord Jesus. If you believe, you will receive whatever you ask for in prayer (Mathew 21:22-24). Have faith in God," Jesus answered. "Truly I tell you, if anyone says to this mountain, 'Go, throw yourself into the sea,' and does not doubt in their heart but believes that what they say will happen, it will be done for them. Therefore, I tell you, whatever you ask for in prayer, believe that you have received it, and it will be yours. And when you stand praying, if you hold anything against anyone, forgive them, so that your Father in heaven may forgive you your sins."(Mark 11:22-25).

Faith is the animating feature of prayer. Prayer is not just words that operate automatically by articulation, it is an interaction of faith.

**Show Respect**. Show respect by humbling yourself

before God and by glorifying him in your thoughts, words, deeds, and attitude. Show respect by identifying and keeping your "Upper Room" sacred! But when you pray, go into your room, close the door, and pray to your Father, who is unseen. Then your Father, who sees what is done in secret, will reward you (Mathew 6:6). Your upper room can be a place in your home or a church or simply an uplifted heart! Your "Upper Room" is a place where you retreat into the conscious presence of God to renew, reflect, refresh, meditate and reinvigorate on the word of God! (Acts 1:12-14). Your Upper room is a place you go to while rejoicing (Psalm 112:1). Though God is everywhere and always with us, we must intentionally experience God's presence through his word, thanksgiving, and gratitude. Whatever or wherever your "Upper Room" is, know that whenever you enter that room, you leave transformed! The upper room experience is an encounter with the holy spirit! After the last supper, the disciples left the upper room as ministers of the Eucharist (Mathew 26:17-30). At Pentecost, the disciples left the upper room as courageous preachers of the gospel (John 20:19-23)

**Invite the Holy Spirit.** When you pray, always remember to invite, and welcome the holy spirit into your private space by opening the door of your heart and receiving his mighty presence. Surrender yourself to his peace, calmness, fire and let his presence overwhelm and transform you.

**Show Gratitude.** When you pray, show gratitude by thanking God for what he has done, what he is doing, and what he is still to do! Show gratitude by thanking him for the good, the bad and the ugly that has happened to you, because We know that all things work together for the good of those who love God, who are called according to his purpose (Romans 8:28).

**Sing unto the Lord.** Praising and worshipping God in prayer through singing is pleasing to God. We praise and worship him for who He is and for all His wonderful works, especially for His grace in accepting us and saving us (Eph. 1:5-7). God invites praise of all kinds from His creation. Praise is so important to God that Jesus said if people do not praise God, even the " stones will cry out " (Luke 19:40). Mahatma Gandhi's take on prayer and singing unto God.

*"Worshipping God is singing the praise of God. Prayer is a confession of one's unworthiness and weakness. God has a thousand names, or rather, He is Nameless. We may worship or pray to Him by whichever name that pleases us. Some call Him Rama, some Krishna, others call Him Rahim, and yet others call Him God. That faith is nothing but a living, wide awake consciousness of God within. He who has achieved that faith wants nothing. Bodily diseased he is spiritually healthy, physically poor, he rolls in spiritual riches. All-Powerful and Omniscient knows our innermost feelings and responds to us according to our deserts. Worship or prayer, therefore, is not to be performed with the lips, but with the heart. And the prayers of those whose tongues are nectared but whose hearts are full of poison are never heard. He, therefore, who would pray to God, must cleanse his heart."*

**Seek God's will.** God's will for us all is in His Word, Intentions, Love and Legacy in Christ Jesus. God's Word communicates His Intentions to us! His Intentions reveal his Love for us! His Love guarantees a Heavenly Legacy for us in Christ Jesus. When you pray, seek God's will to be done on earth as it is in Heaven. Seek God's will to be fulfilled in your life by surrendering your will to God's will. Obey what you already know to be God's will and invite God's input through the holy spirit. The will of God is

God's divine plan for humanity. For I know the plans I have for you," declares the LORD, "plans to prosper you and not to harm you, plans to give you hope and a future *(Jeremiah 29:11*. Trust in the LORD with all your heart and lean not on your own understanding; in all your ways submit to him, and he will make your paths straight (Proverbs 3:5-6) God created us with the intention that we will always live in His presence. We must be connected to Him because it is only in Him that life exists. God is our natural environment. GOD without man is always GOD but man without GOD is nothing!

**Read or quote from the Bible.** Praying the Word means reading (or reciting) Scripture in a spirit of prayer and letting the meaning of the verses inspire our thoughts and become our prayer. Throughout the Old and New Testaments, we find instances of God's people "praying the Word" by quoting Scripture in their prayers. You may want to begin your prayer by reading a passage from the Bible which has significance and meaning to you or quoting a verse or passage that matters to you at that moment! God's word is powerful alive and active. Sharper than any double-edged sword, it penetrates even to dividing soul and spirit, joints, and marrow; it judges the thoughts and attitudes of the heart (Hebrew 4:12). Hearing God's word will increase your faith. Consequently, faith comes from hearing the message, and the message is heard through the word about Christ (Romans 10:17). As we read through God's word, we should be aware that God will lead us to many more wonderful passages that can inspire a deeper prayer life. If the principles in the verses we read apply to a situation in our life, then its important to pray through those truths while applying them to our specific situation.

**Make Room to Listen During Prayers**. When we

are in God's presence in prayers and thanksgiving, we must always create room to listen to the spirit minister to us! And when you pray, do not keep on babbling like pagans, for they think they will be heard because of their many words (Mathew 6:7). "Prayer is not asking. Prayer is putting oneself in the hands of God, at His disposition, and listening to His voice in the depth of our hearts." (Mother Teresa). One of the key things to listening to God and responding to God's call is to tap into that God-inspired desire within oneself to please God, to respond to God in love, to reverence and stand in awe of God. One of the best ways to do this is to spend time with God as much as we can and determinedly listen. Always remember that nothing you tell God is new to him, he knows everything about you, you are better off listening and obeying more than speaking. Do not merely listen to the word, and so deceive yourselves. Do what it says **(James 1:22).**

**Thank God.** When we pray, we must thank God for his amazing power and work in our lives, his goodness, mercy, love, and grace upon our lives. In everything, we must give him thanks as part of his will for us in Christ Jesus **(1 Thessalonians 5:18).** We must give thanks to God with all our heart; and also tell of all His wonderful deeds **(Psalm 9:1)**. God our heavenly father and the creator of heaven and earth has given us everything we have and provides for us every day. It is therefore a show of gratitude to thank him always especially when we are having a conversation with him in prayer. Saying thank you to God tells Him that we love Him and that we acknowledge Him as the source of all we are and have.

**Ask for forgiveness**. It is comforting coming to God knowing that if we ask, it shall be given unto us **(Mathew 7:7)** God bases how He forgives us by the forgiveness we extend to others! So, when we pray, we must ask God to forgive our sins and to help us forgive those that have sinned against us (**Mathew 6:12**).

**Ask for guidance**. When we pray and ask for guidance, God will deliver us from all that is evil (**Mathew 6:13**). Also, when we call on him in the day of trouble; he will deliver us, and we will honor him (**Psalm 50:15**).

**Pray for others**. Therefore, confess your sins to each other and pray for each other so that you may be healed. The prayer of a righteous person is powerful and effective (**James 5:16**). God blesses those who pray for others. After Job had prayed for his friends, the LORD restored his fortunes and gave him twice as much as he had before (**Job 42:10**).

**Trust and Obey.** Trust God's WILL through reliance and confident expectation. Obedience is a fundamentally important key to receiving answers from prayers. We must consistently walk in obedience to His commands by obeying whatever the spirit leads us to do. We must always pray to God to give us a humble heart to submit to his will and be flexible for the Holy Spirit's guidance in our lives so that we can prosper. The Holy Spirit reveals God's thoughts, teaches, and guides believers into all truth, including knowledge of what is to come. To be happy in Christ Jesus, we must trust and obey. Do not merely listen to the word, and so deceive yourselves. Do what it says (**James 1:22**). We must trust the wisdom and perfection of God's will for our lives by surrendering our will for God's will. God Desires our willing obedience motivated by love and gratitude! We must trust God's WILL for our lives because he has a plan for us (**Jeremiah 29:11**). We must trust God's WILL for our lives because he is our refuge (**Psalm 62:6-8**). We must trust God's WILL for our lives because he will fight for us **(Exodus 14:14)**. We must trust God's WILL for our lives because He thinks about us **(Psalm 139:17)**. We must trust God's WILL for our lives because He is always with us **(Mathew 29:20)**. We must trust God's WILL for our lives because he knows every single one of us by name **(Isaiah 43:1)**. We must trust God's WILL for our lives because He loved us first before we ever loved him **(1 John 4:19)**.

## Chapter Sixteen
# How Does God Answer our Prayers?

**God answers every** prayer according to his will for us in Christ Jesus. God always answers every single prayer—just not always the way you want—and he does it in one of three ways. It is generally accepted that there are three ways God answers prayer: 'Yes', 'No' and 'Wait'. 'Yes' is the answer we crave for. And it is always the answer when we ask God to forgive our sins in Jesus' Name. God has promised that, when we ask for things that are in accordance with His will for our lives, He will give us what we ask for **(1 John 5:14–15).** God is never going to give you anything that is hurtful or bad for you. After all, if even imperfect parents know how to give good gifts to their kids, won't God, who is good and perfect, do even more for you? He is ready to answer your prayer—in his own perfect time and way.

God answers our prayers according to his ordained will in each of our lives. God answers our prayers according to his Word, Intentions, Love, and Legacy. He answers our prayers according to his wisdom, and his holiness. Prayers are answered according to the power of God within us as confirmed by the spirit of God that lives in us. If we pray for something that dishonors God or is not His will for us, He is unlikely to give what we ask for. God's wisdom far exceeds our own, and we must trust that His answers to our prayers are the best possible solutions. God answers our prayers when we receive and acknowledge his Son Jesus Christ before others **(Mathew 10:32).**

## WHAT THE BIBLE SAYS ABOUT HOW GOD ANSWERS OUR PRAYERS

> **Luke 11:11-13:** Which of you fathers, if your son asks for a fish, will give him a snake instead? Or if he asks for an egg, will give him a scorpion? If you then, though you are evil, know how to give good gifts to your children, how much more will your Father in heaven give the Holy Spirit to those who ask him!"
> **John 5:30:** By myself I can do nothing; I judge only as I hear, and my judgment is just, for I seek not to please myself but him who sent me
> **John 15:7:** If you remain in me and my words remain in you, ask whatever you wish, and it will be done for you.
> **John 15:16:** You did not choose me, but I chose you and appointed you so that you might go and bear fruit-fruit that will last-and so that whatever you ask in my name the Father will give you.
> **1 John 5:14-15:** This is the confidence we have in approaching God: that if we ask anything according to his will, he hears us. And if we know that he hears us-whatever we ask-we know that we have what we

asked of him.

**Isaiah 65:24:** Before they call, I will answer; while they are still speaking, I will hear.

**Hebrews 11:6:** And without faith it is impossible to please God, because anyone who comes to him must believe that he exists and that he rewards those who earnestly seek him.

**1 Thessalonians 5:17:** pray continually, give thanks in all circumstances; for this is God's will for you in Christ Jesus.

**I Corinthians 10:13:** No temptation has overtaken you except what is common to mankind. And God is faithful; he will not let you be tempted beyond what you can bear. But when you are tempted, he will also provide a way out so that you can endure it.

**James 4:3:** When you ask, you do not receive, because you ask with wrong motives, that you may spend what you get on your pleasures.

**James 5:13-18:** Is anyone among you in trouble? Let them pray. Is anyone happy? Let them sing songs of praise. Is anyone among you sick? Let them call the elders of the church to pray over them and anoint them with oil in the name of the LORD. And the prayer offered in faith will make the sick person well; the LORD will raise them up. If they have sinned, they will be forgiven. Therefore, confess your sins to each other and pray for each other so that you may be healed. The prayer of a righteous person is powerful and effective. Elijah was a human being, even as we are. He prayed earnestly that it would not rain, and it did not rain on the land for three and a half years. Again, he prayed, and the heavens gave rain, and the earth produced its crops.

**Mathew 10:32:** Whoever acknowledges me before others, I will also acknowledge before my Father in heaven.

**Micah 7:7-8:** But as for me, I watch in hope for the LORD, I wait for God my Savior; my God will hear me. Do not gloat over me, my enemy! Though I have fallen, I will rise. Though I sit in darkness, the LORD will be my light.

**Psalm 37:4-6:** Take delight in the LORD, and he will give you the desires of your heart. Commit your way to the LORD; trust in him and he will do this: He will make your righteous reward shine like the dawn, your vindication like the noonday sun.

**Psalm 50:14-15:** Sacrifice thank offerings to God, fulfill your vows to the Most High, ¹⁵and call on me in the day of trouble; I will deliver you, and you will honor me."

**Psalm 55:22:** Cast your cares on the LORD and he will sustain you; he will never let the righteous be shaken.

**2 Chronicles 7:14:** If my people, who are called by my name, will humble themselves and pray and seek my face and turn from their wicked ways, then I will hear from heaven, and I will forgive their sin and will heal their land."

*Chapter Seventeen*

# THE ROLE OF THE HOLY SPIRIT IN OUR PRAYER LIVES

**THE HOLY SPIRIT** is the divine power of God (**Zechariah 4:6; Micah 3:8, 2 Timothy 1:7, Acts 1:8, Romans 15:13, Romans 15:19**). The Holy Spirit reveals God's thoughts, teaches, and guides believers into all truth, including knowledge of what is to come. The Holy Spirit also helps Christians in their weakness and intercedes for them. Through the power of the Holy Spirit, believers are saved, filled, sealed, and sanctified.

The Holy Spirit is the Life and Power of Jesus Christ Himself, which He has received from God the Father. Jesus Christ began His ministry in the power of the Spirit (**Luke 4:14, Luke 1:35, Acts 10:38**). Every work of Jesus on earth was orchestrated by the Holy Spirit. Jesus was raised from the death by the Holy Spirit (**Romans 1:4**). Christ declared that after his ascension, he would send to his church, as his crowning gift, the comforter, who was to take his place. The Holy Spirit lives in us, we are God's temple.

God inspires and guides His prophets and servants to reveal his plan through the power of the Holy Spirit. Prophecy never came by the will of man, but holy men of God spoke as they were moved by the Holy Spirit **(2 Peter 1:21, Ephesians 3:5)**. The Holy Spirit is not only the Spirit of God the Father; it is also "the Spirit of Christ" **(Romans 8:9; Philippians 1:19; 1 Peter 1:11)**. The Holy Spirit dwells within Christians, leading and enabling us to be children of God **(Romans 8:14)**.

**The Holy Spirit as our Companion.** The Holy Spirit dwells in every obedient believer in Jesus Christ to accompany, assist and comfort. Don't you know that you yourselves are God's temple and that God's Spirit dwells in your midst? **(1 Corinthians 3:16)**.

**The Holy Spirit as a Legal Counsel and Teacher:** But the Advocate, the Holy Spirit, whom the Father will send in my name, will teach you all things and will remind you of everything I have said to you **(John 14:26)**.

**The Holy Spirit as a Special Gift from Jesus Christ.** Jesus Christ gave the gift of the holy spirit to us through the powers vested in him by God almighty. The Holy Spirit on his part has the power to bless everyone of us with special spiritual gifts as he deems fit. "But very truly I tell you, it is for your good that I am going away. Unless I go away, the Advocate will not come to you; but if I go, I will send him to you" **(John 16:7)** But when the kindness and love of God our Savior appeared, he saved us, not because of righteous things we had done, but because of his mercy. He saved us through the washing of rebirth and renewal by the Holy Spirit, whom he poured out on us generously through Jesus Christ our Savior, **(Titus 3:4-6)**.

"Now to each one the manifestation of the Spirit is

given for the common good. To one there is given through the Spirit a message of wisdom, to another a message of knowledge by means of the same Spirit, to another faith by the same Spirit, to another gifts of healing by that one Spirit, to another miraculous powers, to another prophecy, to another distinguishing between spirits, to another speaking in different kinds of tongues, and to still another the interpretation of tongues. All these are the work of one and the same Spirit, and he distributes them to each one, just as he determines" (1 Corinthians 12:7-11)

**The Holy Spirit as a Convictor**. One role of the Holy Spirit is the conviction of sin. If we are temples of God, the presence of the holy spirit within us, will convict us, and others, of sin. We will feel more affinity towards those who, like us, long for more conviction, repentance, and the power of God to live a life that will stand the test of fire. When he comes, he will prove the world to be in the wrong about sin and righteousness and judgment **(John 16:8)**.

**The Holy Spirit as a Source of Wisdom and Revelation.** These are the things God has revealed to us by his Spirit. The Spirit searches all things, even the deep things of God. For who knows a person's thoughts except their own spirit within them? In the same way no one knows the thoughts of God except the Spirit of God **(1 Corinthians 2:10-11)**. I keep asking that the God of our LORD Jesus Christ, the glorious Father, may give you the Spirit of wisdom and revelation, so that you may know him better **(Ephesians 1:17)**. All Scripture is God-breathed and is useful for teaching, rebuking, correcting, and training in righteousness **(2 Timothy 3:16)**.

**The Holy Spirit as a Source of Power.** The holy spirit empowers and strengthens when it dwells within us.

But you will receive power when the Holy Spirit comes on you; and you will be my witnesses in Jerusalem, and in all Judea and Samaria, and to the ends of the earth **(Acts 1:8)**. After they prayed, the place where they were meeting was shaken. And they were all filled with the Holy Spirit and spoke the word of God boldly **(Acts 4:31)**. The holy spirit fills the believer and empowers the believer **(Act 2:4)**. The Holy Spirit anoints the believer **(1 John 2:27)**. The Holy Spirit sanctifies the believer **(1 Peter 1:23)**.

**The Holy Spirit as a Guarantor of Sonship**. In this adoption confirmation the holy Spirit fulfils a powerful role as He is called the 'Spirit of sonship'. Because of our 'sonship' status there is no reason at all to have any anxious fears for God. For those who are led by the Spirit of God are the children of God. The holy spirit adopts us as children of God **(2 Timothy 2:19-21)**.

The Spirit you received does not make you slaves, so that you live in fear again; rather, the Spirit you received brought about your adoption to sonship. And by him we cry, "Abba, Father." The Spirit himself testifies with our spirit that we are God's children **(Romans 8:14-16)**.

**The Holy Spirit as a Guide**. The Holy Spirit is a trustworthy guide. The Holy Spirit, the Spirit of truth, helps believers discern between what is true and what is not; what is wise and what is unwise. But when he, the Spirit of truth, comes, he will guide you into all the truth. He will not speak on his own; he will speak only what he hears, and he will tell you what is yet to come **(John 16:13)**.

**The Holy Spirit as an Intercessor.** The Holy Spirit intercedes for us on earth by praying for us. While Jesus is praying for us in heaven, the Holy Spirit is praying for us here on earth in our hearts. In the same way, the

Spirit helps us in our weakness. We do not know what we ought to pray for, but the Spirit himself intercedes for us through wordless groans. And he who searches our hearts knows the mind of the Spirit, because the Spirit intercedes for God's people in accordance with the will of God **(Romans 8:26-27)**.

**The Holy Spirit as an Interpreter of Scriptures**. The role of the Holy Spirit in the Interpretation of Scripture is to guide us to the truth contained within it. The Spirit assists us in interpretation by guiding us to truth, convincing us that it is true, and helping us understand and appropriate truth to our own faith and way of life **(1 Corinthians 9:14, 2 Peter 1:20)**.

**The Holy Spirit as a Life Giver**. As the Giver of Life, the Holy Spirit empowers us believers. The Holy Spirit is present and active in our lives, bringing about life. The Spirit of God has made me; the breath of the Almighty gives me life (Job 33:4). But if Christ is in you, then even though your body is subject to death because of sin, the Spirit gives life because of righteousness. And if the Spirit of him who raised Jesus from the dead is living in you, he who raised Christ from the dead will also give life to your mortal bodies because of his Spirit who lives in you (Romans 8:10-11).

**The Holy Spirit as a Sanctifier**. The Holy Spirit is called holy because of His work as our sanctifier. Sanctification is a lifelong process involving the cooperative work of both the believer and the Holy Spirit. But we ought always to thank God for you, brothers and sisters loved by the LORD, because God chose you as first fruits to be saved through the sanctifying work of the Spirit and through belief in the truth (2 Thessalonians 2:13, 1Peter 1:23).

You, my brothers, and sisters, were called to be free. But do not use your freedom to indulge the flesh; rather, serve one another humbly in love. For the entire law is fulfilled in keeping this one command: "Love your neighbor as yourself." If you bite and devour each other, watch out or you will be destroyed by each other. So, I say, walk by the Spirit, and you will not gratify the desires of the flesh. For the flesh desires what is contrary to the Spirit, and the Spirit what is contrary to the flesh. They conflict with each other, so that you are not to do whatever you want. But if you are led by the Spirit, you are not under the law. The acts of the flesh are obvious: sexual immorality, impurity, and debauchery; idolatry and witchcraft; hatred, discord, jealousy, fits of rage, selfish ambition, dissensions, factions, and envy; drunkenness, orgies, and the like. I warn you, as I did before, that those who live like this will not inherit the kingdom of God (Galatians 5:13-21).

But the fruit of the Spirit is love, joy, peace, forbearance, kindness, goodness, faithfulness, gentleness, and self-control. Against such things there is no law. Those who belong to Christ Jesus have crucified the flesh with its passions and desires. Since we live by the Spirit, let us keep in step with the Spirit (Galatians 5:22-25).

*Chapter Eighteen*

# WHAT IS GODLY SUCCESS?

**IT IS IMPORTANT** to note here that Godly success is never limited to Spiritual success only, it also includes Family success, Business success, Personal success, Health success and Legacy success. As a youth mentor for many years now, the answer I get from every single youth when asked What they want to do with their lives, points to the fact that they all want success. I am still to meet an individual who is not aspiring to become successful in whatever they do. Even those that are not in pursuit of a specific career path yet talk and dream of a successful future. The youths tell me all the time how they Want to be Successful so they can have things and do anything to look or feel as if they have made it.

But my question is this, what do we as believers and followers of Christ consider to be what success is and what it should look like for someone patenting their life after God? Are we embracing the worldly definition of success as displayed in our parking garage, walk-in closets, billboards, television, Hollywood, bank accounts and picture-perfect family portraits? The world has used a whole lot of visuals and mantras to define success but not a true definition of Godly success.

Everyone wants success, but the best version of success is Godly success. Be my guest....

**What is Success?** To better understand a Godly success, let us start by understanding the meaning of success. The Oxford Dictionary defines success as the accomplishment of an aim or purpose, or the attainment of popularity or profit or a person or thing that achieves desired aims or attains prosperity. Merriam-Webster Dictionary defines it as "the fact of getting or achieving wealth, respect, or fame."

### Success as Viewed by Famous People Who Consider Themselves as Successful

- Late Coach John Wooden, defined success as an attitude in the following words: "Success is peace of mind, which is a direct result of self-satisfaction in knowing you made the effort to do your best to become the best that you are capable of becoming."
- Zappos CEO Tony Hsieh defines success as "living in accordance with your values."
- Maya Angelou defines success in the following words: "Success is liking yourself, liking what you do, and liking how you do it."
- British politician Winston Churchill thought that success is being relentless. He defined success in the following words: "Success is going from failure to failure without losing enthusiasm."
- Billionaire Richard Branson believes success is about engagement. He defines success in the following words: "The more you're actively and practically

engaged, the more successful you will feel."
- Spiritual teacher Deepak Chopra believes success is a matter of constant growth. Success in life could be defined as the continued expansion of happiness and the progressive realization of worthy goals. Chopra writes in "<u>The Seven Spiritual Laws of Success</u>."
- Inventor Thomas Edison recognized that success is a grind. He defined success; thus, "Success is 1% inspiration, 99% perspiration."
- Popular author Stephen Covey said that the definition of success is deeply individual. "If you carefully consider what you want to be said of you in the funeral experience, you will find your definition of success."
- Huffington Post founder Arianna Huffington says that money and power are not enough to define success. She adds that "a third measure of success that goes beyond the two metrics of money and power, and consists of four pillars: well-being, wisdom, wonder, and giving."
- For Bill Gates the American business magnate, software developer, investor, philanthropist and co-founder of Microsoft Corporation, success is defined by two factors: making a difference and taking care of the people closest to you.
- Albert Einstein had a formula for success. Can you believe that? One of the greatest minds of all time developed a math formula for success! Einstein said, "If A equals success, then the formula is: $A=X+Y+Z$.
- X is work, Y is play, Z is keep your mouth shut." Einstein learned the value of work, play, quietness, and solitude for success.

## WHAT THEN IS GODLY SUCCESS?

It is important to note here that success is never limited to financial success only, it also includes Family success, Business success, Personal success, Health success, Legacy success, and spiritual success.

**What is Business Success?** Business success is defined as achieving the short- and long-term objectives you have set for your business endeavor and moving a little bit closer to achieving your long-term vision with every action the organization is involved with. Business success comes from using an idea to create something of real value and using that something to improve yourself and the lives of others.

**What is Family Success?** Family success is attained when families promote the emotional, physical, and social welfare of individual family members by providing the best opportunities to learn and grow. Family success can be a source of strength and joy throughout life for all members of that family. Our homes and families are the foundation for happiness and success in life.

**What is Health Success?** Good health we all agree is essential for a successful life Health success is a state of physical, mental, and social well-being in which disease and infirmity are absent or where disease and infirmity are professionally managed.

**What is Legacy Success?** This type of success can only be appropriately measured after we are death and gone! It is measured in terms of what we leave behind for the next generation when we are called to be with the Lord! Legacy success is achieved whenever one lives behind more than what he inherited from the previous generation. Jesus left his teachings and twelve disciples as part of his legacy and today we have more than 3 billion Christians who have accepted the teachings and leadership of Christ Jesus.

**What is Spiritual Success?** Spiritual success is about who we are in Christ Jesus. It is portrayed by our faith, character, and integrity. Spiritual success enables us to live in such a way that even those who do not know God, will come to know God because they know us! Spiritual success comes with spiritual awareness, love and support of others, spiritual courage, spiritual discipline, spiritual integrity, and spiritual relentlessness.

**What is Personal Success?** Personal success is the realization of your Godly ordained purpose. It includes the realization of personal goals such as loving and being loved, discipline, faith, spiritual growth, strength, self-confidence, integrity. Personal success is what you aspire to achieve for yourself: emotionally, physically and in your personal relationships. personal relationships. It is what you aspire to achieve for yourself: emotionally, physically and in your personal relationships. Every other form of success is part of our personal success!

**Godly success is about who is looking but worldly success is about how it looks.** Godly Success is obedience to God, empowered by the Spirit of God, motivated by love for God, and directed toward the advancement of the kingdom of God. Success begins with obeying God's command to repent and believe in Jesus Christ (Mark 1:15; Acts 19:4; 20:21). When a person receives Jesus Christ, they also receive the Holy Spirit (Ephesians 1:13–14; 4:30; Romans 8:9; 2 Timothy 1:14).

**Godly Success is God given and Godly inspired.** In Joshua 1:8, the Bible commands us to meditate on the word of God and put in into practice to ensure our success. So many other references align to this scripture and the sum I gathered from them is that Godly Success is a reward for obedience to God. God has commanded us that once we obey His will for our lives, He would happily bless us with Godly Success

**Godly Success is a reward for obedience to God.** Godly Success is manifested in supernatural favors because of obedience to God. God, all throughout the Bible and all throughout time, has rewarded His people for their obedience. When we follow His will and plan for our lives, things are sure to be well with us. So many times, throughout scripture men who did not appear successful in the eyes of society but were obedient to God were advanced tremendously and used to show forth His glory. We have seen this played out in the lives of Moses, Noah, Abraham, Daniel, David, Ester, Nehemiah, Joseph, Jesus, and His disciple. When you focus on God and depend on him for guidance you are guaranteed Godly Success. The people of Noah's day thought he had lost his mind and he was socially shunned upon. But when the flood came, he and his family were the only ones who had good success. David was counted out by his family because by the looks of it, he was not considered to be king of a nation. But David, who was a man after God's own heart would rise from that obscure opinion to be a great warrior and king. When it comes to real Success its nothing like when God establishes you. If you are giving your best effort, living according to His plan, and seeking Him daily, you will be blessed with Godly success. If we are obedient to God, He will give us things we need and want in His timing. One day of His favor is worth more than 1,000 days of our labor. People always talk about the secrets of Success, but the number one secret is just obedience to God, and you will always have an unfair advantage (Supernatural Favor).

**Godly success is about favor not labor.** Whenever we think about Success we think about hustling, working hard, grind mode and doing what it takes to gain money, notoriety and to be on top. With this mantra, Godly Success compared to the world system may seem weird. It goes against the grain because it requires not just a physical effort, but it is also a lesson in faith.

**Godly Success is eternal and has no limits.** The best thing about Godly Success is that we have it now and we can have it later. Success that everyone pursues, along with its material possessions and accolades are limited to this life only. Solomon, the wisest man that ever lived reminds me of a lot of successful people who were not able to fill life's void with things. In the opening of Ecclesiastes, Solomon, I can imagine, surrounded by extreme wealth and everything a man would ever want sums it all up by saying "everything is meaningless, a chasing after the wind." Jesus said, "What Good is it for a man to gain the whole world and lose His own soul?" Mark 16:26 .

**Godly success is God's original intent for our lives.** Adam and Eve, in the beginning were given a good thing. Everything was in a perfect, untampered state, and when God made them, He saw that they were good (Genesis 1:31). Adam worked, because work is a God given thing. He did not toil. There is a difference. If they were obedient to God and did not eat from the forbidden tree, they were given Good Success and had 100% favor with God. It was only when man was cursed, the toil began.

**Godly success is about value not valuables.**

**Godly success is about spiritual health not earthly wealth.**

**Godly success is all about God and not all about you.**

**Godly Success is the fulfillment of God's Will for our life.** God's will for our lives is intertwined in the very word **WILL**! His will for us all is in His Word, Intentions, Love and Legacy! When God's Word communicates His Intentions to us, His Intentions reveal his Love for us, His Love guarantees a Heavenly Legacy for us in Christ Jesus, and his Legacy for us is warranted when we seek first his kingdom and his righteousness (Mathew 6:33), Godly success is achieved!

*Chapter Nineteen*

# THE GODLY PRAYER AND GODLY SUCCESS OF HANNAH
## THE PROPHETESS

**HANNAH IS ONE** of the most poignant characters in the Bible. She was one of two wives of a man named Elkanah who lived "in the hill country of Ephraim" near Shiloh. The other wife of Elkanah, Peninnah, had children, but Hannah had no child. Because of this, Hannah was very grieved. She desperately desired a child but could not conceive. Hannah's prayer is a remarkable passage of Scripture containing a song of praise with prophetic and messianic significance.

In her deep anguish Hannah prayed to the Lord, weeping bitterly. And she made a vow, saying, "Lord Almighty, if you will only look on your servant's misery and remember me, and not forget your servant but give her a son, then I will give him to the Lord for all the days of his life, and no razor will ever be used on his head."

As she kept on praying to the Lord, Eli observed her

mouth. Hannah was praying in her heart, and her lips were moving but her voice was not heard. Eli thought she was drunk and said to her, "How long are you going to stay drunk? Put away your wine." "Not so, my lord," Hannah replied, "I am a woman who is deeply troubled. I have not been drinking wine or beer; I was pouring out my soul to the Lord. Do not take your servant for a wicked woman; I have been praying here out of my great anguish and grief." Eli answered, "Go in peace, and may the God of Israel grant you what you have asked of him." **(1Samuel 1:10-17).**

Found in **1 Samuel 2:1-10**, Hannah's prayer eloquently celebrates the holiness reverence and sovereignty of God. Her prayer acknowledges that God is all knowing (omniscience), all present (omnipresent), and all powerful (omnipotent).

**1 Samuel 2:1-10:** Then Hannah prayed and said: "My heart rejoices in the LORD; in the LORD my horn is lifted high. My mouth boasts over my enemies, for I delight in your deliverance. There is no one holy like the LORD; there is no one besides you; there is no Rock like our God. Do not keep talking so proudly or let your mouth speak such arrogance, for the LORD is a God who knows, and by him deeds are weighed. The bows of the warriors are broken, but those who stumbled are armed with strength. Those who were full hire themselves out for food, but those who were hungry are hungry no more. She who was barren has borne seven children, but she who has had many sons' pines away. The LORD brings death and makes alive; he brings down to the grave and raises up. ⁷The LORD sends poverty and wealth; he humbles, and he exalts. He raises the poor from the dust and lifts the needy from the ash heap; he seats them with princes and has them inherit a throne of honor. For the foundations of the earth are the LORD's; on them he has set the world. He will guard the feet of his faithful servants, but the wicked will be silenced in the place of darkness. It is not by strength that one prevails; those who oppose the LORD will be broken. The Most High will thunder from heaven; the LORD will judge the ends of the earth. He will give strength to his king and exalt the horn of his anointed."

**Hannah's Answered Prayer**. In the course of time Hannah became pregnant and gave birth to a son. She named him Samuel, saying, "Because I asked the LORD for him." When her husband Elkanah went up with all his family to offer the annual sacrifice to the LORD and to fulfill his vow, Hannah did not go. She said to her husband, "After the boy is weaned, I will take him and present him before the LORD, and he will live there always.**"(1 Samuel 1:20-22)**. Hannah kept her word as she had vowed. After Samuel was weaned, she presented him to Eli the priest **(1 Samuel 1:24)**.

*Chapter Twenty*

# THE GODLY PRAYER AND GODLY SUCCESS OF MOSES

**MOSES' PRAYER FOR Israel in the Wilderness (Exodus 32:9-14)**: Moses pleads with God to preserve his own name and character and not destroy Israel. I have seen these people," the LORD said to Moses, "and they are a stiff-necked people. Now leave me alone so that my anger may burn against them and that I may destroy them. Then I will make you into a great nation." But Moses sought the favor of the LORD his God. "LORD," he said, "why should your anger burn against your people, whom you brought out of Egypt with great power and a mighty hand? Why should the Egyptians say, 'It was with evil intent that he brought them out, to kill them in the mountains and to wipe them off the face of the earth'? Turn from your fierce anger; relent and do not bring disaster on your people. Remember your servants Abraham, Isaac and Israel, to whom you swore by your own self: 'I will make your descendants as numerous as the stars in the sky and I will give your descendants all this land I promised them, and it will be their inheritance forever.'" Then the LORD relented and did not bring on his people the disaster he had threatened.

In this prayer, Moses prayed for God's Presence, prayed according to God's will and promises and he prayed for knowledge about God. He pleaded, reminded, asked, and prayed for others. He got God's attention and God did not bring on his people the disaster he had threatened! His prayer acknowledges that God is all knowing (omniscience), all present (omnipresent), and all powerful (omnipotent).

## Chapter Twenty-One
# THE GODLY PRAYER AND GODLY SUCCESS OF NOAH

**NOAH'S PRAYER OF obedience in the face of a deadly flood (Genesis 6-9):** The greatest prayer of Noah was silence and obedience to God! Noah's recorded encounter with God is an example of the fact that prayer is not supposed to be a recited chant. Prayer is talking and listening to God and the greatest prayer sometimes is simply being patient, obedient and silently listening to God's commands. But Noah found favor in the eyes of the LORD **(Genesis 6:8)**. And Noah did all that the Lord commanded him. And Noah and his sons and his wife and his sons' wives entered the ark to escape the waters of the flood." **(Genesis 7:5-7)**.

Then God blessed Noah and his sons, saying to them, "Be fruitful and increase in number and fill the earth. The fear and dread of you will fall on all the beasts of the earth, and on all the birds in the sky, on every creature that moves along the ground, and on all the fish in the sea; they are given into your hands. Everything that lives and moves about will be food for you. Just as I gave you the green plants, I now give you everything. "But you must not eat meat that has its lifeblood still in it. And for your lifeblood I will surely demand an accounting. I will demand an accounting from every animal. And from each human being, too, I will demand an accounting for the life of another human being. "Whoever sheds human blood, by humans shall their blood be shed; for in the image of God has God made mankind **(Genesis 9:1-6).**

*Chapter Twenty-two*

# THE GODLY PRAYER AND GODLY SUCCESS OF ABRAHAM

**ABRAHAM'S PRAYER FOR Sodom (Genesis 18:16-33):** "When the men got up to leave, they looked down toward Sodom, and Abraham walked along with them to see them on their way. Then the Lord said, "Shall I hide from Abraham what I am about to do? Abraham will surely become a great and powerful nation, and all nations on earth will be blessed through him. For I have chosen him, so that he will direct his children and his household after him to keep the way of the Lord by doing what is right and just, so that the Lord will bring about for Abraham what he has promised him."

Then the Lord said, "The outcry against Sodom and Gomorrah is so great and their sin so grievous that I will go down and see if what they have done is as bad as the outcry that has reached me. If not, I will know."

The men turned away and went toward Sodom, but Abraham remained standing before the Lord. Then Abraham approached him and said: "Will you sweep away the righteous with the wicked? What if there are fifty righteous people in the city? Will you really sweep it away and not spare the place for the sake of the fifty righteous people in it? Far be it from you to do such a thing—to kill the righteous with the wicked, treating the righteous and the wicked alike. Far be it from you! Will not the Judge of all the earth do, right?" The Lord said, "If I find fifty righteous people in the city of Sodom, I will spare the whole place for their sake." Then Abraham spoke up again: "Now that I have been so bold as to speak to the Lord, though I am nothing but dust and ashes, what if the number of the righteous is five less than fifty? Will you destroy the whole city for lack of five people?" "If I find forty-five there," he said, "I will not destroy it." Once again, he spoke to him, "What if only forty are found there?" He said, "For the sake of forty, I will not do it."

Then he said, "May the Lord not be angry, but let me speak. What if only thirty can be found there?" He answered, "I will not do it if I find thirty there." Abraham said, "Now that I have been so bold as to speak to the Lord, what if only twenty can be found there?" He said, "For the sake of twenty, I will not destroy it." Then he said, "May the Lord not be angry, but let me speak just once more. What if only ten can be found there?" He answered, "For the sake of ten, I will not destroy it." Then the Lord had finished speaking with Abraham, he left, and Abraham returned home.

Abraham's prayer for Sodom is a conversation and negotiation between God and Abraham. It is an amazing revelation of the faith of one man in the justice of Almighty God and an incredible boldness of a mere human before the Creator of the Universe. Abraham seems to stand before God alone yet wields significant influence over God's actions.

*Chapter Twenty-Three*
# THE GODLY PRAYER AND GODLY SUCCESS OF DANIEL

DANIEL (GOD IS my judge) was the second son of David. His mother was Abigail (**1 Chronicles 3:1**) Daniel was one of the great prophets who wrote the Bible book of Daniel. Daniel's prayer is intense, acknowledges sin, and the crucial facts that God is all knowing (omniscience), all present (omnipresent), and all powerful (omnipotent).Well, this is a prayer that really got God's attention because of its sincerity, intensity and earnesty. This powerful prayer is found in the Book of **Daniel 9:1-17.**

"In the first year of Darius son of Xerxes (a Mede by descent), who was made ruler over the Babylonian kingdomin the first year of his reign, I, Daniel, understood from the Scriptures, according to the word of the LORD given to Jeremiah the prophet, that the desolation of Jerusalem would last seventy years. So, I turned to the LORD God and pleaded with him in prayer and petition, in fasting, and in sackcloth and ashes. I prayed to the LORD my God and confessed: "LORD, the great and awesome God, who keeps his covenant of love with those who love him and keep his commandments, we have sinned and done wrong. We have been wicked and have rebelled; we have turned away from your commands and laws. We have not listened to your servants the prophets, who spoke in your name to our kings, our princes, and our ancestors, and to all the people of the land. "LORD, you are righteous, but this day we are covered with shame-the people of Judah and the inhabitants of Jerusalem and all Israel, both near and far, in all the countries where you have scattered us because of our unfaithfulness to you. We and our kings, our princes and our ancestors are covered with shame, LORD, because we have sinned against you. The LORD our God is merciful and forgiving, even though we have rebelled against him; we have not obeyed the LORD our God or kept the laws he gave us through his servants the prophets. All Israel has transgressed your law and turned away, refusing to obey you. "Therefore, the curses and sworn judgments written in the Law of Moses, the servant of God, have been poured out on us, because we have sinned against you. You have fulfilled the words spoken against us and against our rulers by bringing on us great disaster. Under the whole heaven nothing has ever been done like what has been done to Jerusalem. Just as it is written in the Law of Moses, all this disaster has come on us, yet we have not sought the favor of the LORD our God by turning from our sins and giving attention to your truth. The LORD did not hesitate to bring the disaster on us, for the LORD our God is righteous in everything he does; yet we have not obeyed him. "Now, LORD our God, who brought your people out of Egypt with a mighty hand and who made for yourself a name that endures to this day, we have sinned, we have done wrong. LORD, in keeping with all your righteous acts, turn away your anger and your wrath from Jerusalem, your city, your holy hill. Our sins and the iniquities of our ancestors have made Jerusalem and your people an object of scorn to all those around us. "Now, our God, hear the prayers and petitions of your servant. For your sake, LORD, look with favor on your desolate sanctuary." (**Daniel 9:1-17**).

**Daniels Answered Prayer.** God's answer is sent immediately. We read in **Daniel 10:12** that God sends His reply the moment He hears our prayers. "Then he said to me, "Do not fear, Daniel, for from the first day that you set your heart to understand, and to humble yourself before your God, your words were heard; and I have come because of your words." Daniels prayer of confession and petition is answered, but certainly not in a way Daniel would have expected. God sent Gabriel, His angel, to give Daniel understanding and insight into the vision he had received, enabling him to see the near future in perspective.

*Chapter Twenty-Four*

# THE GODLY PRAYER AND GODLY SUCCESS OF DAVID

**DAVID'S PRAYER FOR Pardon and Confession of Sin (Psalm 51):** David prayed this prayer after committing adultery with Bathsheba.

"Have mercy on me, O God, according to your unfailing love; according to your great compassion blot out my transgressions. Wash away all my iniquity and cleanse me from my sin. For I know my transgressions, and my sin is always before me. Against you, you only, have I sinned and done what is evil in your sight; so, you are right in your verdict and justified when you judge. Surely, I was sinful at birth, sinful from the time my mother conceived me. Yet you desired faithfulness even in the womb; you taught me wisdom in that secret place. Cleanse me with hyssop, and I will be clean; wash me, and I will be whiter than snow. Let me hear joy and gladness; let the bones you have crushed rejoice. Hide your face from my sins and blot out all my iniquity. Create in me a pure heart, O God, and renew a steadfast spirit within me. Do not cast me from your presence or take your Holy Spirit from me. Restore to me the joy of your salvation and grant me a willing spirit, to sustain me. Then I will teach transgressors your ways, so that sinners will turn back to you. Deliver me from the guilt of bloodshed, O God, you who are God my Savior, and my tongue will sing of your righteousness. Open my lips, Lord, and my mouth will declare your praise. You do not delight in sacrifice, or I would bring it; you do not take pleasure in burnt offerings. My sacrifice, O God, is a broken spirit; a broken and contrite heart you, God, will not despise. May it please you to prosper Zion, to build up the walls of Jerusalem. Then you will delight in the sacrifices of the righteous, in burnt offerings offered whole; then bulls will be offered on your altar."

**David's Psalm of Surrender (Psalm 139):** David struggles with God's intense knowledge of him, marvels at God's intricate formation of him in his mother's womb, and then prays a prayer of surrender to God's way of searching, knowing, probing and refining His children.

"You have searched me, LORD, and you know me. You know when I sit and when I rise; you perceive my thoughts from afar. You discern my going out and my lying down; you are familiar with all my ways. Before a word is on my tongue you, LORD, know it completely. You hem me in behind and before, and you lay your hand upon me. Such knowledge is too wonderful for me, too lofty for me to attain. Where can I go from your Spirit? Where can I flee from your presence? If I go up to the heavens, you are there; if I make my bed in the depths, you are there. If I rise on the wings of the dawn, if I settle on the far side of the sea, even there your hand will guide me, your right hand will hold me fast. If I say, "Surely the darkness will hide me and the light become night around me," even the darkness will not be dark to you; the night will shine like the day, for darkness is as light to you. For you created my inmost being you knit me together in my mother's womb. I praise you because I am fearfully and wonderfully made; your works are wonderful; I know that full well. My frame was not hidden from you when I was made in the secret place, when I was woven together in the depths of the earth. Your eyes saw my unformed body; all the days ordained for me were written in your book before one of them came to be. How precious to me are your thoughts, God! How vast is the sum of them! Where I to count them, they would outnumber the grains of sand— when I awake, I am still with you. If only you, God, would slay the wicked! Away from me, you who are bloodthirsty! They speak of you with evil intent; your adversaries misuse your name. Do I not hate those who hate you, LORD, and abhor those who are in rebellion against you? I have nothing but hatred for them; I count them my enemies. Search me, God, and know my heart; test me and know my anxious thoughts. See if there is any offensive way in me and lead me in the way everlasting."

May God help us to be willing to pray like David, fast, wait for God's direction, then act on the wisdom He provides. May we be ever faithful to pray for all those in authority, for those who need someone to speak up on their behalf, for those who are being pressed down or persecuted.

David's prayer is intense, acknowledges sin, surrenders and confesses that God is all knowing (omniscience), all present (omnipresent), and all powerful (omnipotent).

*Chapter Twenty-Five*
# THE GODLY PRAYER AND GODLY SUCCESS OF ESTHER

Esther, in the book of Esther, was a biblical heroine who saved the Jewish people. She is recognized mostly for her strength, bravery, and dignity. She was chosen by the Persian King Ahasuerus to be his wife in a contest, not knowing she was a Jew. When the king's right-hand man, Haman, came up with a plan to kill the Jews, Esther's uncle found her and pleaded with her to spare Israel. Even though she was his wife, she knew she was not allowed to approach him without invitation, and if she did, it could end in death. But she believed she was chosen by God to save her own people and agreed to go in front of the king anyway and won his favor and her people were saved. She did not let her fear or position stand in her way. As noted in the book of Esther, Queen Esther fasted and prayed for three days and by God's special grace, she was able to win the kings heart and save her people the Jews. Then she took off the clothes she had been wearing and put on her splendid robes again. In all her royal splendor, she prayed again to her God and savior, who sees everything.

**Esther knew when her action mattered**. *"For if you remain silent at this time, relief and deliverance for the Jews will arise from another place, but you and your father's family will perish…" Esther 4:14.*

**Esther understood the power of fasting.** *"Then Esther sent this reply to Mordecai: 'Go, gather together all the Jews who are in Susa, and fast for me. Do not eat or drink for three days, night or day. I and my maids will fast as you do. When this is done, I will go to the king, even though it is against the law. And if I perish, I perish,'" Esther 4:15-16.*

*Chapter Twenty-Six*
# The Godly Prayer and Godly Success of Nehemiah

**Nehemiah's Prayer for Success** *(Nehemiah 1:5:10):* Nehemiah hears of the suffering of the returned exiles. After grieving in fasting and prayer, he prays for success -- and commits himself to God's will for his life.

Then I said; "Lord, the God of heaven, the great and awesome God, who keeps his covenant of love with those who love him and keep his commandments, let your ear be attentive and your eyes open to hear the prayer your servant is praying before you day and night for your servants, the people of Israel. I confess the sins we Israelites, including myself and my father's family, have committed against you. We have acted very wickedly toward you. We have not obeyed the commands, decrees, and laws you gave your servant Moses. "Remember the instruction you gave your servant Moses, saying, 'If you are unfaithful, I will scatter you among the nations, but if you return to me and obey my commands, then even if your exiled people are at the farthest horizon, I will gather them from there and bring them to the place I have chosen as a dwelling for my Name.' "They are your servants and your people, whom you redeemed by your great strength and your mighty hand. Lord, let your ear be attentive to the prayer of this your servant and to the prayer of your servants who delight in revering your name. Give your servant success today by granting him favor in the presence of this man."

*Chapter Twenty-Seven*

# THE GODLY PRAYER AND GODLY SUCCESS OF ELIJAH

**THE PROPHET ELIJAH** is one of the most intriguing people in the Bible, and God used him during an important time in Israel's history to oppose a wicked king and bring revival to the land.

**Elijah was as human as we are with a big Faith in God**. when he prayed earnestly that no rain would fall, none fell for three and a half years! At the usual time for offering the evening sacrifice, Elijah the prophet walked up to the altar and prayed, "O Lord, God of Abraham, Isaac, and Jacob, prove today that you are God in Israel and that I am your servant. Prove that I have done all this at your command. Immediately the fire of the Lord flashed down from heaven and burned up the young bull, the wood, the stones, and the dust. It even licked up all the water in the trench! *(***1 Kings 18:36, 38).** Then, when he prayed again, the sky sent down rain and the earth began to yield its crops **(James 5:17-18**).

**Elijah learned to be completely dependent on**

**God**. After Elijah's first confrontation with King Ahab, God sent him to the Kerith Brook. There Elijah sat, no food, no provisions. But God saw his needs. It was there, with everything stripped away, that God sent ravens to bring him food. So, Elijah did as the Lord told him and camped beside Kerith Brook, east of the Jordan. The ravens brought him bread and meat each morning and evening, and he drank from the brook *(*1 **Kings 17:5-6**).

**Elijah prayed vehemently with Expectation.** Elijah knew that sometimes an answer does not come immediately. He knew that we must pray until we see the breakthrough. And he was committed for the long haul.

Elijah climbed to the top of Mount Carmel and bowed low to the ground and prayed with his face between his knees. Then he said to his servant, "Go and look out toward the sea." The servant went and looked, then returned to Elijah and said, "I didn't see anything." Seven times Elijah told him to go and look. Finally, the seventh time, his servant told him, "I saw a little cloud about the size of a man's hand rising from the sea." Then Elijah shouted, "Hurry to Ahab and tell him, 'Climb into your chariot and go back home. If you do not hurry, the rain will stop you!'" And soon the sky was black with clouds. A heavy wind brought a terrific rainstorm, and Ahab left quickly for Jezreel *(*1 **KINGS 18:41-46**).

**Elijah was completely in tune with God**. He listened for Yahweh's voice, and he walked in obedience (**1 Kings 18:36**). He prayed in agreement with what God asked of him. And his prayers pointed the world back to God.

Elijah's Godly Prayers and Godly Success are also the credentials of Elijah's divine mission and the evidence that God deals with men. Elijah went to the top of Mount

Carmel to pray for rain. As he started to pray, he tells his servant to look toward the sea for any sign of rain **(1 Kings 18:43)**. Elijah did not just pray. He also looked for results actively. So often it is easy to go through the motion of prayer without really expecting anything to happen.

*Chapter Twenty-Eight*

# The Godly Prayers and Godly Success of Job

**Job is the** central figure of the Book of Job in the Bible. The characters in the Book of Job consist of Job, his wife, his three friends (Bildad, Eliphaz, and Zophar), a man named Elihu, God, and angels (one of whom is named Satan). The story of Job is a powerful tale of testing the devotion and fortitude of the human will. In this epic wager between God and the Devil, discover how Job reacts to the shocking curses inflicted upon him and what we can learn from his incredible example of remaining faithful through suffering.

The first thing the Bible tells us about Job is that he was righteous and godly, "blameless and upright," a man who "feared God and shunned evil" **(Job 1:2)**. Job was not only righteous, but also wealthy. We also know Job was a man greatly tested by God and even more greatly blessed by God. He was concerned about the spiritual welfare of his children **(Job 1:4-5)**.

**Job's Prayer when he heard that all ten of his**

**children had been killed (Job 1:18-19).** At this, Job got up and tore his robe and shaved his head. Then he fell to the ground in worship and said: *"Naked I came from my mother's womb, and naked I will depart. The Lord gave and the Lord has taken away; may the name of the Lord be praised."* In all this, Job did not sin by charging God with wrongdoing. **(Job 1:20-22)**

**Job's Prayer when his health comes under attack.** *"Oh, that I might have my request, that God would grant what I hope for, that God would be willing to crush me, to let loose his hand and cut off my life! Then I would still have this consolation- my joy in unrelenting pain- that I had not denied the words of the Holy One. "What strength do I have, that I should still hope? What prospects, that I should be patient? Do I have the strength of stone? Is my flesh bronze? Do I have any power to help myself now that success has been driven from me?* **"(Job 6:8-13)**

**Job Submits Himself to God.** Then Job replied to the LORD: "I know that you can do all things; no purpose of yours can be thwarted. You asked, 'Who is this that obscures my plans without knowledge?' Surely, I spoke of things I did not understand, things too wonderful for me to know. You said, 'Listen now, and I will speak; I will question you, and you shall answer me.' My ears had heard of you but now my eyes have seen you. Therefore, I despise myself and repent in dust and ashes." **(Job 42:1-6)**

**God blesses Job Double.** Then Jehovah gave back to Job, twice as much as he had before. And Jehovah blessed the last part of Job's life more than the first part; and he had fourteen thousand sheep, six thousand camels, a thousand yoke of oxen, and a thousand asses. He also had seven sons and three daughters. And after this Job lived a hundred and forty years **(Job 42:10-17)**

*Chapter Twenty-Nine*

# THE GODLY PRAYERS AND GODLY SUCCESS OF JEREMIAH

**JEREMIAH WAS A** prophet of the seventh century B.C. who came from Anathoth, a town a short distance from Jerusalem. Most of his prophetic career was spent in the vicinity of Jerusalem. Jeremiah began to prophesy in the reign of King Josiah of Judah. Jeremiah was called to be a prophet while he was still a youth. Like many prophets, Jeremiah repeatedly asked God for guidance on behalf of others in the Israelite community **(Jeremiah 37 and 42).** He also brought his own troubles to the Lord, lamenting both his calling and its context in history. Jeremiah regularly prayed for the people of Israel. Like Moses before him, he regularly interceded for Israel with God, pleading with the Lord not to bring upon them the tragedy that He had promised.

**The Godly Prayer of Jeremiah.** You are always righteous, LORD, when I bring a case before you. Yet I would speak with you about your justice: Why does the way of the wicked prosper? Why do all the faithless live at ease? You have planted them, and they have taken root; they grow and bear fruit. You are always on their lips but far from their hearts. Yet you know me, LORD; you see me and test my thoughts about you. Drag them off like sheep to be butchered! Set them apart for the day of slaughter! How long will the land lie parched and the grass in every field be withered? Because those who live in it are wicked, the animals and birds have perished. Moreover, the people are saying, "He will not see what happens to us." "If you have raced with men on foot and they have worn you out, how can you compete with horses? If you stumble in safe country, how will you manage in the thickets by the Jordan? Your relatives, members of your own family—even they have betrayed you; they have raised a loud cry against you. Do not trust them, though they speak well of you. "I will forsake my house, abandon my inheritance; I will give the one I love into the hands of her enemies. My inheritance has become to me like a lion in the forest. She roars at me; therefore, I hate her. Has not my inheritance become to me like a speckled bird of prey that other birds of prey surround and attack? Go and gather all the wild beasts; bring them to devour. Many shepherds will ruin my vineyard and trample down my field; they will turn my pleasant field into a desolate wasteland. It will be made a wasteland, parched and desolate before me; the whole land will be laid waste because there is no one who cares. Over all the barren heights in the desert destroyers will swarm, for the sword of the LORD will devour from one end of the land to the other; no one will be safe. They will sow wheat but reap thorns; they will wear themselves out but gain nothing. They will bear the shame of their harvest because of the LORD's fierce anger." This is what the LORD says: "As for all my wicked neighbors who seize the inheritance I gave my people Israel, I will uproot them from their lands and I will uproot the people of Judah from among them. But after I uproot them, I will again have compassion and will bring each of them back to their own inheritance and their own country. And if they learn well the ways of my people and swear by my name, saying, 'As surely as the LORD lives'—even as they once taught my people to swear by Baal—then they will be established among my people. But if any nation does not listen, I will completely uproot and destroy it," declares the LORD **(Jeremiah 12:1-17)**.

Jeremiah's prayer teaches us that through prayer, we can express all to God, all our deepest thoughts, all our deepest longings, all our deepest frustrations without fear. His prayer also teaches us how to trust, obey and influence others for God.

A crucial element of this prayer is God's initial response to Jeremiah's doubts and reluctance regarding his call to be a prophet to the nations earlier on. In **Jeremiah 1:7-10** God addresses Jeremiah's concerns; First, God assures Jeremiah that he will tell the prophet where to go and what to say. Second, God promises to deliver Jeremiah from all danger. And third, God reminds Jeremiah that he has given him the authority to carry out his ministry.

That said, if you ask me, these was assurance enough to enable Jeremiah to pray such bold prayers beginning his prayers with expressions like "O Lord" **(Jeremiah 17:13; Jeremiah 20:7; Jeremiah 12:1; Jeremiah 18:19)**, and not only did he petition God to be present and attentive to his prayer **(Jeremiah 18:19)**, he also confessed his belief and confidence in God's presence.

*Chapter Thirty*

# THE GODLY PRAYER AND GODLY SUCCESS OF JOSHUA

HIS NAME WAS Hoshea the son of Nun, of the tribe of Ephraim, but Moses called him Joshua (**Numbers 13:16**)**,** the name by which he is commonly known. According to the Bible he was born in Egypt prior to the Exodus. According to the books of Exodus, Numbers and Joshua, he was Moses' assistant and became the leader of the Israelite tribes after the death of Moses. In **Numbers 13:1-16**, and after the death of Moses, he led the Israelite tribes in the conquest of Canaan and allocated the land to the tribes.

**Joshua's Prayer for the Sun and Moon to Stand Still.** Joshua was pursuing a coalition of enemy kings who had attacked their Gibeonite allies which were under their protection. Because he did not want the enemy to get away and have to fight them again, Joshua prayed so that he could continue pursuing his enemies.

**Joshua 10:12-13**. On the day the Lord gave the Amorites over to Israel, Joshua said to the Lord in the presence of Israel: "Sun, stand still over Gibeon, and you, moon, over the Valley of Aijalon."So the sun stood still, and the moon stopped, till the nation avenged itself on its enemies, as it is written in the Book of Jashar. The sun stopped in the middle of the sky and delayed going down about a full day.

Joshua's heroic prayer acknowledged the omniscience, omnipotence, and omnipresence of God. Through prayer, we acknowledge that God is all knowing (omniscience), all present (omnipresent), and all powerful (omnipotent). Omnipotence means that God is in total control of himself and his creation. His omnipresence is a presence both in place and in time.

Joshua was a humble student of Moses who knew the Source and the Secret to Success and trusted and obeyed God. Joshua was a young leader who stood for principle and never followed the Crowd. He is one respected bible hero of mine who exercised heroic faith with success.

Joshua's name means **"Jehovah is salvation."**. Like the other Israelites, he had been born into slavery in the land of Egypt. Joshua was empowered and commissioned by God to succeed Moses after Moses' death **(Deuteronomy 31:23; Joshua 1:5)**. But before Joshua was an exemplary leader, he was first a faithful follower.

**The Godly Success of Joshua**. The Godly Success of Joshua is wrapped up in In **Joshua 1:1-9** where God encourages Joshua in his new role as leader of Israel. These verses lay out a program for the success of Joshua and the Israelites in taking over the Promised Land and thriving there.

**Joshua 1:1-9:** After the death of Moses the servant of the Lord, the Lord said to Joshua son of Nun, Moses' aide: "Moses my servant is dead. Now then, you and all these people, get ready to cross the Jordan River into the land I am about to give to them—to the Israelites. I will give you every place where you set your foot, as I promised Moses. Your territory will extend from the desert to Lebanon, and from the great river, the Euphrates—all the Hittite country—to the Mediterranean Sea in the west. No one will be able to stand against you all the days of your life. As I was with Moses, so I will be with you; I will never leave you nor forsake you. Be strong and courageous, because you will lead these people to inherit the land, I swore to their ancestors to give them. "Be strong and very courageous. Be careful to obey all the law my servant Moses gave you; do not turn from it to the right or to the left, that you may be successful wherever you go. Keep this Book of the Law always on your lips; meditate on it day and night, so that you may be careful to do everything written in it. Then you will be prosperous and successful. Have I not commanded you? Be strong and courageous. Do not be afraid; do not be discouraged, for the Lord your God will be with you wherever you go."

*Chapter Thirty-One*

# THE GODLY PRAYERS AND GODLY SUCCESS OF NAOMI

**WHO WAS NAOMI?** Naomi lived during the time of the Judges. She was the wife of a man named Elimelech, and they lived in Bethlehem with their two sons, Mahlon and Kilion. When a famine hits Judea, Elimelech and Naomi and their two boys relocate to Moab (**Ruth 1:1**). There, Mahlon and Kilion marry two Moabite women, Orpah and Ruth. After about ten years, tragedy strikes. Elimelech dies, and both of Naomi's sons also die, leaving Naomi, Ruth, and Orpah widows (**Ruth 1:3–5**). Naomi, hearing that the famine in Judea was over, decides to return home (**Ruth 1:6**). Orpah stays in Moab, but Ruth chooses to move to the land of Israel with Naomi. The book of Ruth is the story of Naomi and Ruth returning to Bethlehem and how Ruth married a man named Boaz and bore a son, Obed, who became the grandfather of David and the ancestor of Jesus Christ.

The name *Naomi* means "sweet, pleasant," which gives us an idea of Naomi's basic character. We see her giving her blessing to Ruth and Orpah when she tells them to return to their mothers' homes so that they might find new husbands: she kisses them and asks that the Lord deal kindly with them (**Ruth 1:8–14**). But her heartache in Moab was more than Naomi could bear. When she and

Ruth arrive in Bethlehem, the women of the town greet Naomi by name, but she cries, "Don't call me Naomi. . .. Call me Mara because the Almighty has made my life very bitter. I went away full, but the Lord has brought me back empty. Why call me Naomi? The Lord has afflicted me; the Almighty has brought misfortune upon me" (**Ruth 1:20–21**). The name *Mara* means "bitter." The cup of affliction is a bitter cup, but Naomi understood that the affliction came from the God who is sovereign in all things. Little did she know that from this bitter sorrow great blessings would come to her, her descendants, and the world through Jesus Christ.

Ruth meets a local landowner, **Boaz,** who is very kind to her. Naomi again recognizes the providence of God in providing a **kinsman-redeemer** for Ruth. Naomi declares that the Lord "has not stopped showing his kindness to the living and the dead." (**Ruth 2:20**). Seeing God's hand in these events, Naomi encourages Ruth to go to Boaz as he slept in the threshing floor in order to request that he redeem her and her property. Naomi's concern was for Ruth's future, that Ruth would gain a husband and provider (**Ruth 3**).

Naomi's bitterness is turned to joy. In the end, she gains a son-in-law who would provide for both her and Ruth. She also becomes a grandmother to Ruth's son, Obed. Then the women of Bethlehem say to Naomi, "Praise be to the Lord, who this day has not left you without a guardian-redeemer. May he become famous throughout Israel! He will renew your life and sustain you in your old age. For your daughter-in-law, who loves you and who is better to you than seven sons, has given him birth"(**Ruth 4:14–15**). Naomi was no longer Mara. Her life again became sweet and pleasant, blessed by God.

**Naomi's Prayers.** Her prayers are found in the Bible Book of Ruth. In chapter 1 Naomi utters **a prayer** for her widowed daughters-in-law, Orpah and Ruth. She also prays for the rich landowner Boaz in Chapter two.

**Naomi's Prayer for Ruth and Orpah (Ruth 1:9)** "The Lord grant that you may find rest, each of you in the house of her husband!" Then she kissed them, and they lifted their voices and wept. At the end both women (Ruth and Orpah) remarry.

**Naomi's Prayer for Boaz (Ruth 2:20)**. "May he be blessed by the Lord, whose kindness has not forsaken the living or the dead!" Naomi also said to her, "The man is a close relative of ours, one of our redeemers." Naomi prays again for Boaz, that he would be repaid for showing such kindness to Ruth. By the stories end, Boaz is blessed with a wife and a child.

It is important to note here that even though Naomi was bitter an even accused God of afflicting her and bringing misfortune upon her,(**Ruth 1:20–21), she never gave up on God!**

Naomi's life illustrates the power of God to bring something good out of bitter circumstances and the importance of praying Godly prayers. At her lowest moment she prayed for others. She prayed for her daughters in laws and for Boaz. Both Ruth and Orpah finally got married. Despite all Naomi still believed in the Omnipresence, Omniscience, and Omnipotence of God! At the end, her faith, love for others and obedience to God was greatly rewarded.

*Chapter Thirty-Two*

# THE GODLY PRAYERS AND GODLY SUCCESS OF JESUS

**JESUS, ALSO REFERRED** to as Jesus of Nazareth and Jesus Christ, was a first-century Jewish preacher and religious leader. He is the central figure of Christianity and is widely described as the most influential person in history. Christian doctrines include the belief that Jesus was conceived by the Holy Spirit, through a virgin named Mary, performed miracles, founded the Church, died by crucifixion as a sacrifice to achieve atonement for sin, rose from the dead, and ascended into Heaven, from where he will return. Most Christians believe Jesus enables people to be reconciled to God. My dear children, I write this to you so that you will not sin. But if anybody does sin, we have an advocate with the Father-Jesus Christ, the Righteous One **(1 John 2:1).**

Jesus was the only person in history who did everything right—not only in saving the world but also in daily life. He brought significance into everything he did, and by following his example we can learn to live the same way. Jesus was the greatest leader and the most influential person ever. As noted in **Hebrews 5:7,** during the days of Jesus' life on earth, he offered up prayers and petitions with fervent cries and tears to the one who could save him from death, and he was heard because of his reverent submission. Therefore, he is able to save completely those who come to God through him, because he always lives to intercede for them **(Hebrews 7:25).** For Christ did not enter a sanctuary made with human hands that was only a copy of the true one; he entered heaven itself, now to appear for us in God's presence **(Hebrews 9:24).**

### THE GODLY PRAYERS OF JESUS CHRIST.

Jesus prayed without ceasing. He prayed all the time. In the New Testament Gospels, we see Jesus praying often – day and night, and sometimes all through the night.

**God Prayed during his Baptism.** When all the people were being baptized, Jesus was baptized too. And as he was praying, heaven was opened, and the Holy Spirit descended on him in bodily form like a dove. And a voice came from heaven: "You are my Son, whom I love; with you I am well pleased."**(Luke 3:21-22)**

**Jesus Prays before choosing his Apostles.** One of those days Jesus went out to a mountainside to pray and spent the night praying to God. When morning came, he called his disciples to him and chose twelve of them, whom he also designated apostles Simon (whom he named Peter), his brother Andrew, James, John, Philip, Bartholomew, Matthew, Thomas, James son of Alphaeus, Simon who was called the Zealot, Judas son of James, and Judas Iscariot, who became a traitor **(Luke 6:12-16).**

**Jesus prays after the healing of a leper**. But Jesus

often withdrew to lonely places and prayed (**Luke 5:16**). He understood the power of solitude in prayers (**Matthew 14:22-23, Mark 1:35-39**). One day Jesus was praying in a certain place. When he finished, one of his disciples said to him, "LORD, teach us to pray, just as John taught his disciples (**Luke 11:1**)

**Jesus listened and obeyed the Holy Spirit when he prayed.** Then Jesus was led by the Spirit into the wilderness to be tempted by the devil (**Matthew 4:1**).

**Jesus Fasted for Forty Days and forty Nights.** Then Jesus was led up by the Spirit into the wilderness to be tempted by the devil. And when He had fasted forty days and forty nights, afterward He was hungry (**Matthew 4:1-2.**).

**Jesus teaches his disciples how to pray with the Lord's Prayer.** This, then, is how you should pray: 'Our Father in heaven, hallowed be your name, your kingdom come, your will be done, on earth as it is in heaven. Give us today our daily bread. And forgive us our debts, as we also have forgiven our debtors. And lead us not into temptation but deliver us from the evil one.' (**Matthew 6:9-13**)

**Jesus prays after being rejected by certain cities in Galilee.** At that time Jesus said, "I praise you, Father, LORD of heaven and earth, because you have hidden these things from the wise and learned and revealed them to little children." (**Matthew 11:25**).

**Jesus prays as He healed a deaf man.** There some people brought to him a man who was deaf and could hardly talk, and they begged Jesus to place his hand on him. After he took him aside, away from the crowd, Jesus put his fingers into the man's ears. Then he spit and touched the man's tongue. He looked up to heaven and with a deep sigh said to him, "Ephphatha!" (which means

"Be opened!"). At this, the man's ears were opened, his tongue was loosened, and he began to speak plainly. Jesus commanded them not to tell anyone. But the more he did so, the more they kept talking about it. People were overwhelmed with amazement. "He has done everything well," they said. "He even makes the deaf hear and the mute speak **(Mark 7:32-37)**

**Jesus prays before feeding 4000 people.** He told the crowd to sit down on the ground. When he had taken the seven loaves and given thanks, he broke them and gave them to his disciples to distribute to the people, and they did so **(Mark 8:6)**.

**Jesus prayed over little children.** People were bringing little children to Jesus for him to place his hands on them, but the disciples rebuked them. When Jesus saw this, he was indignant. He said to them, "Let the little children come to me, and do not hinder them, for the kingdom of God belongs to such as these. Truly I tell you, anyone who will not receive the kingdom of God like a little child will never enter it." And he took the children in his arms, placed his hands on them and blessed them **(Mark 10:13-16)**.

**Jesus prays during His transfiguration.** About eight days after Jesus said this, he took Peter, John, and James with him and went up onto a mountain to pray. As he was praying, the appearance of his face changed, and his clothes became as bright as a flash of lightning. Two men, Moses, and Elijah, appeared in glorious splendor, talking with Jesus. They spoke about his departure, which he was about to bring to fulfillment at Jerusalem. Peter and his companions were very sleepy, but when they became fully awake, they saw his glory and the two men standing with him. As the men were leaving Jesus, Peter said to him, "Master, it is good for us to be here. Let us put up three shelters-one for you, one for Moses and one for Elijah." (He did not know what he was saying.) While he was speaking, a cloud appeared and covered them, and they were afraid as they entered the cloud. A voice came from the cloud, saying, "This is my Son, whom I have chosen; listen to him **(Luke 9:28-35)**

Praying after hearing the report of the seventy the seventy-two returned with joy and said, "LORD, even the demons submit to us in your name." He replied, "I saw Satan fall like lightning from heaven. I have given you authority to trample on snakes and scorpions and to overcome all the power of the enemy; nothing will harm you. However, do not rejoice that the spirits submit to you, but rejoice that your names are written in heaven." At that time Jesus, full of joy through the Holy Spirit, said, "I praise you, Father, LORD of heaven and earth, because you have hidden these things from the wise and learned, and revealed them to little children. Yes, Father, for this is what you were pleased to do **(Luke 10:17-21)**.

**Jesus prays in the garden of Gethsemane.** They went to a place called Gethsemane, and Jesus said to his disciples, "Sit here while I pray." He took Peter, James, and John along with him, and he began to be deeply distressed and troubled (**Mark 14:32-42**).

**Jesus prays over Jerusalem.** Jerusalem, Jerusalem, you who kill the prophets and stone those sent to you, how often I have longed to gather your children together, as a hen gathers her chicks under her wings, and you were not willing. Look, your house is left to you desolate. For I tell you, you will not see me again until you say, 'Blessed is he who comes in the name of the LORD. (**Matthew 23:37-39**). As he approached Jerusalem and saw the city, he wept over it and said, "If you, even you, had only known on this day what would bring you peace-but now it is hidden from your eyes. The days will come upon you when your enemies will build an embankment against you and encircle you and hem you in on every side. They will dash you to the ground, you, and the children within your walls. They will not leave one stone on another, because you did not recognize the time of God's coming to you." (**Luke 19:41-44**).

**Jesus prays in the upper room just before he dies.** While they were eating, Jesus took bread, and when he had given thanks, he broke it and gave it to his disciples, saying, "Take and eat; this is my body." Then he took a cup, and when he had given thanks, he gave it to them, saying, "Drink from it, all of you. This is my blood of the covenant, which is poured out for many for the forgiveness of sins." (**Matthew 26:26-28**).

**Jesus prays for Simon Peter.** Simon, Simon, Satan has asked to sift all of you as wheat. But I have prayed for you, Simon, that your faith may not fail. And when you have turned back, strengthen your brothers." But he replied, "LORD, I am ready to go with you to prison and to death." Jesus answered, "I tell you, Peter, before the rooster crows today, you will deny three times that you know me." (**Luke 22:31-34**).

**Jesus Prays and Accepts God's Will for His Life.** Going a little farther, he fell with his face to the ground and prayed, "My Father, if it is possible, may this cup be taken from me. Yet not as I will, but as you will." Then he returned to his disciples and found them sleeping. "Couldn't you men keep watch with me for one hour?" he asked Peter. "Watch and pray so that you will not fall into temptation. The spirit is willing, but the flesh is weak." He went away a second time and prayed, "My Father, if it is not possible for this cup to be taken away unless I drink it, may your will be done." When he came back, he again found them sleeping, because their eyes were heavy. So, he left them and went away once more and prayed the third time, saying the same thing. Then he returned to the disciples and said to them, "Are you still sleeping and resting? Look, the hour has come, and the Son of Man is delivered into the hands of sinners. Rise! Let us go! Here comes my betrayer!" **(Matthew 26:39-46).**

**Jesus prays for the thieves dividing his clothes while on the cross.** Jesus said, "Father, forgive them, for they do not know what they are doing." And they divided up his clothes by casting lots **(Luke 23:34).**

**Jesus Prays on the Cross before Dying.** About three in the afternoon Jesus cried out in a loud voice, "Eli, Eli, lema sabachthani?" (which means "My God, my God, why have you forsaken me?"). **(Matthew 27:46).**

**Jesus Last Prayer before Dying.** Jesus final words were "Father, into Your hands I commit my spirit" **(Luke 23:46).** Here, Jesus is willingly giving up His soul into the Father's hands, indicating that He was about to die – and that God had accepted His sacrifice. He "offered up Himself unblemished to God" **(Hebrews 9:14).**

**Jesus prays before feeding of 5000 people (John 6:11).** Jesus then took the loaves, gave thanks, and distributed to those who were seated as much as they wanted. He did the same with the fish.

**Jesus praying at Lazarus' grave (John 11:41-42).** So, they took away the stone. Then Jesus looked up and said, "Father, I thank you that you have heard me. [42]I knew that you always hear me, but I said this for the benefit of the people standing here, that they may believe that you sent me."

**Jesus prays and Predicts his Death (John 12:20-28).** Now there were some Greeks among those who went up to worship at the festival. They came to Philip, who was from Bethsaida in Galilee, with a request. "Sir," they said, "we would like to see Jesus." Philip went to tell Andrew; Andrew and Philip in turn told Jesus. Jesus replied, "The hour has come for the Son of Man to be glorified. Very truly I tell you, unless a kernel of wheat falls to the ground and dies, it remains only a single seed. But if it dies, it produces many seeds. Anyone who loves their life will lose it, while anyone who hates their life in this world will keep it for eternal life. Whoever serves me must follow me; and where I am, my servant also will be. My Father will honor the one who serves me. "Now my soul is troubled, and what shall I say? 'Father, save me from this hour'? No, it was for this very reason I came to this hour. Father, glorify your name!" Then a voice came from heaven, "I have glorified it, and will glorify it again."

**Jesus prays at the Ascension** When he had led them out to the vicinity of Bethany, he lifted his hands and blessed them. While he was blessing them, he left them and Great joy. And they stayed continually at the temple, praising God **(Luke 24:50-53).**

### THE KEY ELEMENTS OF THE PRAYER LIFE OF JESUS

- Jesus prayed without ceasing
- Jesus prayed according to the will of God
- Jesus prayed for others
- Jesus obeyed the Holy Spirit
- Jesus fasted for forty days and forty nights
- When He prayed, he also listened to hear from God

- When He prayed, he showed Gratitude
- When he prayed, he praised God
- When he prayed, he asked for guidance
- When he prayed, He thanked God
- When he prayed, he asked for forgiveness for others

**THE GODLY SUCCESS OF JESUS CHRIST.**

Jesus is the greatest leader that ever lived, He became the ultimate sacrifice, a mediator, a perfect example, an outstanding teacher, established his kingdom, and accomplished grace and salvation for mankind. He conquered death (3:16). Jesus's resurrection means death is defeated. When Christ conquered death for us, He removed the "sting of death," sin **(1 Corinthians 15:56)**—that is, we will not be judged by God according to our sins; rather, we will stand before God robed in Christ's own perfect righteousness.

**Jesus is the greatest leader that ever lived**. His ministry was started with just twelve disciples. a humble origin, (a son of a carpenter from the Judean countryside), a short life, (about 33 years), and a very short public career, (about three years). Jesus is the central focus of the world's largest religion and has meant many things to many people since his death almost 2,000 years ago. In addition to mainstream Christianity, Jesus is important in many new religious movements that grew out of Christianity and even in some non-Christian religions such as Islam, the Baha'i Faith, and Cao Dai. Jesus is respected as a wise teacher by many Buddhists, Hindus, some Jews, and even many non-religious people.

**Jesus became the ultimate sacrifice.** Jesus had an existence before he came to this earth **(John. 8: 58,**

**John. 1: 1).** Jesus, the Word (logos), had enjoyed all the splendor of heaven as God **(Philippians 2: 7-8).** Jesus offered himself as a sin offering for all the sins of man **(Hebrew 10: 1-10, 12, 14).** Jesus said, "For this is my blood of the New Testament, which is shed for many for the remission of sins" **(Matthew 26: 28, Acts 2: 38).** All the great men of the world combined could not help man regarding his sins. Jesus is the sacrificial «Lamb of God, which taketh away the sin of the world,» exclaimed John the Baptist **(John. 1: 29).**

**Jesus became the consummate mediator.** A mediator is a go between, one who acts in behalf of two parties, in this case God and man. Jesus is the one and only mediator between God and man (I Tim. 2: 5). Jesus is peculiarly qualified because he is both God and man (Heb. 1: 8, I Tim. 2: 5). Jesus, then, became the entrance to the Father. Hear him: "I am the way, the truth, and the life: no man cometh unto the Father, but by me" (Jn. 14: 6).

**Jesus set the perfect example.** Peter said of Jesus, "…leaving us an example" (I Pet. 2: 21). Jesus is our example in prayer, standing for the truth, and rebuking sinners (Lk. 6: 12; Matt. 4: 4, 7, 10; Matt. 23). Jesus is our exemplar in the matter of service and keeping God's commandments (Jn. 13: 7-16; Jn. 4: 34).

**Jesus was the world's most outstanding teacher (Matt. 5: 2).** Teaching is an act of generosity and Jesus portrayed nothing but generosity in all he did and said. Jesus taught "them as one having authority, and not as the scribes" (Matt. 7: 29). Hence, people then and now are amazed (vs. 28). Jesus' teaching is applicable, practical, and concrete. It is also exclusive, I might add. Hence, to go beyond Jesus' teaching is to forfeit God (2 Jn. 9). Jesus' teaching is also so complete that all other teaching is forbidden

(2 Jn. 10, 11, Gal. 1: 6-10). In addition to the teaching that Jesus personally uttered while on earth, he articulated his will through his apostles (I Cor. 14: 37).

**Jesus established his Kingdom.** The Kingdom was prophesied long before Jesus' advent into this world (Dan. 2 ff). Jesus came at the "fullness of time" (Gal. 4: 4). Jesus promised to build his church or Kingdom and he kept his promise (Matt. 16: 18, 19). The Christians at Colossians had been "translated into the Kingdom of his dear Son" (Col. 1: 13). Some continue to wait on a secular, political Kingdom. Jesus never taught or promised such a kingdom (Jn. 18: 36, 37).

**Jesus accomplished grace and salvation for mankind.** Grace came by Jesus (Jn. 1: 17). Jesus came that man might have life and have it more abundantly (Jn. 10: 10). However, this eternal life is not unconditional. If eternal life or salvation were unconditional, as some teach, all men would be saved. Alas, only a relatively few will be saved (Matt. 7: 13, 14). Man must believe, repent, confess Christ's deity, and be baptized for the remission of sins to appropriate God's grace (Jn. 8: 24, Acts 17: 30, 31, Rom. 10: 9, 10, Acts 2: 38).

*Chapter Thirty-Three*

# GODLY SUCCESS COMES AT A COST AND FOR A CAUSE!

**GODLY PRAYERS ARE** the ladder to Godly success. However, it is important to know that Godly Success comes at a COST and for a CAUSE! God was willing to pay the highest price in the universe to redeem you—the blood of His dear Son. For you know that it was not with perishable things such as silver or gold that you were redeemed from the empty way of life handed down to you from your ancestors, but with the precious blood of Christ, a lamb without blemish or defect(**1 Peter 1:18, 19**). An excellent example of Godly success we can relate to as humans is the example of the Apostle Paul in the Bible. In the following verses he pours out his heart about all what he has been through to be where he is! And that is not all, after all of that he now must use his Godly success to help other people! Also remember that Paul was not perfect in physical health (torn in my flesh) but his spiritual health and success were astounding.

## The Cost of Godly Success

1. **Godly Success Comes with Trials and Tribulations.** Five times I received from the Jews the forty lashes minus one. Three times I was beaten with rods, once I was pelted with stones, three times I was shipwrecked, I spent a night and a day in the open sea, I have been constantly on the move. I have been in danger from rivers, in danger from bandits, in danger from my fellow Jews, in danger from Gentiles; in danger in the city, in danger in the country, in danger at sea; and in danger from false believers. I have labored and toiled and have often gone without sleep; I have known hunger and thirst and have often gone without food; I have been cold and naked. Besides everything else, I face daily the pressure of my concern for all the churches. Who is weak, and I do not feel weak? Who is led into sin, and I do not inwardly burn? If I must boast, I will boast of the things that show my weakness **(2 Corinthians 11:24-30).**
2. **Do Not Go Beyond What Is Written (1 Corinthians 4:6)**. With Godly success you must respect boundaries, the word of God is our guide! Let the boundaries of Scripture be our guide—not religious traditions or modern societal standards. Paul was dealing with competing factions that were vying for prominence in the Corinthian church. Some of these Christians were making determinations merely on opinion and personal preference. Paul reminded them that this must be avoided. The Handbook or Manual for our lives is the Word of God—the Bible. Paul was basically warning us not to add rigid

boundaries where Scripture is silent. Your word is a lamp for my feet, a light on my path **(Psalms 119:105)**.
3. **You are Crucified with Christ.** Being crucified with Christ means that we have a new love. Those who belong to Christ Jesus have crucified the flesh with its passions and desires **(Galatians 5:24)**. I have been crucified with Christ and I no longer live, but Christ lives in me. The life I now live in the body, I live by faith in the Son of God, who loved me and gave himself for me **(Galatians 2:20)**.
4. **Total Obedience to God's Commands**. From Genesis to Revelation, the Bible has a lot to say about obedience. In the story of the Ten Commandments, we see just how important the concept of obedience is to God. **Deuteronomy 11:26-28** sums it up like this: "Obey and you will be blessed. Disobey and you will be cursed." Do not add to what I command you and do not subtract from it but keep the commands of the LORD your God that I give you. **(Deuteronomy 4:2).** Now if you obey God fully and keep His covenant, then out of all nations you will be His treasured possession. Although the whole earth is His **(Exodus 19:15)**. Our obedience is part of our assurance that we truly know God **(1 John 2:3)**.
5. **Unconditional Love for God.** God's love for mankind, as described in the Bible, is clearly unconditional in that He loves because it is His nature to love **(1 John 4:8).** Godly success calls us to Love the LORD our God with all our heart and with all our soul and with all our strength **(Deuteronomy 6:5)**. Loving God with all our heart, soul and

strength means love for God that is, absolute, categorical, complete, express, indubitable, positive, total unequivocal, unquestioning, unreserved, unlimited, unrestricted, and wholehearted. Anyone who loves their father or mother more than God is not worthy of Him; anyone who loves their son or daughter more than God is not worthy of God **(Mathew 10:37).**

6. **Husbands Must love their Wives as Christ Loved the Church.** Godly success calls for husbands to love their wives, just as Christ loved the church and gave himself up for her **(Ephesians 5:25).** Loving your wife as Christ loved the church means having a strong and cordial affection for your wife. It means supporting and encouraging your wife. It means showing respect and honoring your wife in private as well as in public. It means seeking your wife's contentment, satisfaction, and pleasure. It means providing a quiet, constant, and comfortable dwelling for her. It means protecting your wife from all injuries and abuses.

7. **Wives Must Submit to their Husbands.** Godly success calls for wives to submit themselves to their own husbands so that, if any of them do not believe the word, they may be won over without words by the behavior of their wives, when they see the purity and reverence of your lives. Your beauty should not come from outward adornment, such as elaborate hairstyles and the wearing of gold jewelry or fine clothes. Rather, it should be that of your inner self, the unfading beauty of a gentle and quiet spirit, which is of great worth in God's sight. For this is the way the holy women of the past who put their hope

in God used to adorn themselves. They submitted themselves to their own husbands, like Sarah, who obeyed Abraham and called him her LORD. You are her daughters if you do what is right and do not give way to fear **(1 Peter 3:1-6)**.

8. **Children Must Obey their Parents.** Honor your father and your mother, so that you may live long in the land the LORD your God is giving you" **(Exodus 20:12)**. Halfway through the Ten Commandments, God instructs His people to honor their fathers and mothers. Godly success calls for children to obey their parents in the LORD, for this is right **(Ephesians 6:1).** Honor your father and your mother, as the LORD your God has commanded you, so that you may live long and that it may go well with you in the land the LORD your God is giving you **(Deuteronomy 5:16).** For God said, 'Honor your father and mother' and 'Anyone who curses their father or mother is to be put to death **(Matthew 15:4).** Honor your father and mother"- which is the first commandment with a promise- so that it may go well with you and that you may enjoy long life on the earth **(Ephesians 6:2-3).**

9. **You Must Serve God as the Only Master.** Godly success calls us to serve God and not money. We must constantly and consistently live God on the throne and never replace him with money. Godly success calls us to use money but worship God! No one can serve two masters. Either you will hate the one and love the other, or you will be devoted to the one and despise the other **(Mathew 6:24).** No one can serve two masters. Either you will hate the one and love the other, or you will be devoted to the one

and despise the other. You cannot serve both God and money **(Luke 16:13).** Then he said to them all: "Whoever wants to be my disciple must deny themselves and take up their cross daily and follow me **(Luke 9:23)**

**Expect Hatred from Men and the Crown of Life from God.** Christians continue to suffer persecution daily in the hands of others worldwide. Godly success may cause you to be hated by everyone because of me, but the one who stands firm to the end will be saved **(Mathew 10:22).** For it is commendable if someone bears up under the pain of unjust suffering because they are conscious of God **(1 Peter 2:19).** Blessed is the one who perseveres under trial because, having stood the test, that person will receive the crown of life that the LORD has promised to those who love him **(James 1:12).**

### THE CAUSE OF GODLY SUCCESS

1. **Godly success is all for the glory of God!** Godly success calls us to do our best to present ourselves to God as one approved, a worker who does not need to be ashamed and who correctly handles the word of truth **(2Timothy 2:15).** And we know that in all things God works for the good of those who love him, who have been called according to his purpose **(Romans 8:28)**
2. **The Poor and Needy.** Godly success commands us to reach out to the poor and needy. There will always be poor people in the land. Therefore, I command you to be openhanded toward your fellow Israelites who are poor and needy in your

land (**Deuteronomy 15:11**). What should we do then?" the crowd asked. John answered, "Anyone who has two shirts should share with the one who has none, and anyone who has food should do the same."(**Luke 3:10-11**). Whoever is kind to the poor lends to the LORD, and he will reward them for what they have done (**Proverbs 19:17**). Share with the LORD's people who are in need. Practice hospitality (**Romans 12:13**).

3. **Carry each other's burden**. Godly success enables us to carry each other's burdens, and in this way, you will fulfill the law of Christ (**Galatians 6:2**) God is not unjust; he will not forget your work and the love you have shown him as you have helped his people and continue to help them (**Hebrews 6:10**) And do not forget to do good and to share with others, for with such sacrifices God is pleased (**Hebrews 13:16**).

4. **Faith must be accompanied by action.** Give to the one who asks you, and do not turn away from the one who wants to borrow from you (**Mathew 5:42**) What good is it, my brothers, and sisters, if someone claims to have faith but has no deeds? Can such faith save them? Suppose a brother or a sister is without clothes and daily food. [16]If one of you says to them, "Go in peace; keep warm and well fed," but does nothing about their physical needs, what good is it? In the same way, faith by itself, if it is not accompanied by action, is dead (**James 2:14-17**). Heal the sick, raise the dead, cleanse those who have leprosy, drive out demons. Freely you have received; freely give (**Mathew 10:8**).

5. **Love each other as God has loved you.** Godly

success requires love for one another. My command is this: Love each other as I have loved you **(John 15:12)**. Give to the one who asks you, and do not turn away from the one who wants to borrow from you **(Mathew 5:42)** Not looking to your own interests but each of you to the interests of the others **(Philippines 2:4)**. Do not withhold good from those to whom it is due, when it is in your power to act **(Proverbs 3:27)**. In the same way, let your light shine before others, that they may see your good deeds and glorify your Father in heaven **(Mathew 5:16)**.

*Chapter Thirty Four*

# LET JESUS CHRIST BE THE COMPASS FOR OUR LIVES!

**JESUS PRAYED FOR** others, with others, without others and for circumstances. He prayed both prayers of petition and prayers of supplication. It is worth mentioning that Jesus' passionate prayers all share one purpose – to glorify our Heavenly Father. **1 Timothy 2:1** gives us four ways of glorifying our heavenly father as Jesus did. "First of all, then, I urge that supplications, prayers, intercessions, and thanksgivings be made for all people."

**JESUS' PASSIONATE PRAYERS GLORIFIED GOD IN THE FOLLOWING WAYS:**

**He Prayed Prayers of Thanksgiving**. "While they were eating, Jesus took bread, gave thanks and broke it, and gave it to his disciples, saying, 'Take it; this is my body'" (**Mark 14:22**). We see another type of prayer in **Philippians 4:6**: thanksgiving or thanks to God. "With thanksgiving let your requests be made known to God.

**He Prayed Prayers of Faith.** Faith is the substance of things that are hoped for, the evidence of things not yet seen **(Hebrews 11:1)**. "Father, into thy hands I commit my spirit" **(Luke 23:46)**. **James 5:15** says, "And the prayer of faith will save the one who is sick, and the Lord will raise him up." In this context, prayer is offered in faith for someone who is sick, asking God to heal. When we pray, we are to believe in the power and goodness of God **(Mark 9:23)**.

**He Prayed Prayers of Agreement** Jesus taught his disciples how to pray (**Luke11:1-13**), prayed with them **(John 18:1)** and encouraged them to pray together **(Luke 22:40)**. After Jesus' ascension, the disciples "all joined together constantly in prayer" **(Acts 1:14)**. Later, after Pentecost, the early church "devoted themselves" to prayer **(Acts 2:42)**. Their example encourages us to pray with others.

**He prayed prayers of Supplication.** A prayer of supplication is a significant part of a Christian's walk because it proves our designed existence and destiny. Perhaps the best way to approach supplications is to ask God in all honesty as children talking to their kind-hearted Father but ending with "Your will be done" **(Matthew 26:39),** in full surrender to His will. Jesus tells us to ask for our daily bread in **Matthew 6:11. In Luke 18:1-8,** Jesus teaches us not to give up praying for what we need**.** We are to take our requests to God. **Philippians 4:6** teaches, "Do not be anxious about anything, but in everything by prayer and supplication with thanksgiving let your requests be made known to God." Part of winning the spiritual battle is to be "praying at all times in the Spirit, with all prayer and supplication" **(Ephesians 6:18).**

**Jesus Prayed Prayers of Intercession:** Many

times, our prayers include requests for others as we intercede for them. We are told to make intercession "for everyone" in **1 Timothy 2:1**. Jesus serves as our example in this area. The whole of **John 17** is a prayer of Jesus on behalf of His disciples and all believers.

**Jesus Prayed Prayers of Blessing on his Enemies. Jesus** said, "Father, forgive them, for they do not know what they are doing." And they divided up his clothes by casting lots **(Luke 23:34).** Jesus teaches us to pray for blessing on our enemies, not cursing **(Matthew 5:44-48).**

**He prayed prayers of Worship.** The prayer of worship is like the prayer of thanksgiving. The difference is that worship focuses on who God is; thanksgiving focuses on what God has done. Jesus prayed for God to be glorified **(John 17:1-5)**.

After Jesus said this, he looked toward heaven and prayed: *"Father, the hour has come. Glorify your Son, that your Son may glorify you. For you granted him authority over all people that he might give eternal life to all those you have given him. Now this is eternal life: that they know you, the only true God, and Jesus Christ, whom you have sent. I have brought you glory on earth by finishing the work you gave me to do. And now, Father, glorify me in your presence with the glory I had with you before the world began."*

**Jesus Prayed the Prayer of Consecration:** Sometimes, prayer is a time of setting oneself apart to follow God's will. Jesus made such a prayer the night before His crucifixion: "And going a little farther he fell on his face and prayed, saying, '*My Father, if it be possible, let this cup pass from me; nevertheless, not as I will, but as you will*" '**(Matthew 26:39)**.

*Chapter Thirty-Five*

# CONCLUSION

**IN EVERYTHING GIVE THANKS!**

**GIVE THANKS IN** all circumstances; for this is God's will for you in Christ Jesus **(1 Thessalonians 5:18).** The LORD is good to all; he has compassion on all he has made **(Psalm 145:9).** In everything give thanks: for this is the will of God in Christ Jesus concerning you (KJV). Give thanks to the LORD, for he is good; his love endures forever **(I Chronicles 16:34).**

Give thanks to God for every good and perfect gift is from above, coming down from the Father of the heavenly lights, who does not change like shifting shadows **(James 1:17).** Give thanks to God in both good and in bad times, in the night time and in the day time, in the valley and on the mountain, in mourning and in celebration, in wealth and in poverty, in sickness and in good health! For the LORD is good and his love endures forever; his faithfulness continues through all generations **(Psalm 100:5).**

God, all throughout the Bible and all throughout time,

has rewarded His people for their obedience. When we follow His will and plan for our lives, things are sure to be well with us. He made everything good and He wants us to partake in it. God wants us to have the best here and now. He wants us to share in what He has already created and stored for us. He wants us to share in that success here and eternally. So, it is important that in all our work, effort, and pursuit, we understand the proper context so we can be guided accordingly.

Always remember that we were created to worship and give thanks to God. All things are created by God and for Him, and our only answer and show of gratitude is to always thank him no matter what! Taste and see that the LORD is good; blessed is the one who takes refuge in him **(Psalm 34:8)**. It is dishonoring to God when we grumble and complain over His gifts, which includes difficulties and trials. Everything and anything that happens to us, happens for a reason and a season and together it works for our good.

And we know that in all things God works for the good of those who love him, who have been called according to his purpose. **(Romans 8:28).** Always sing to the Lord with praise and thanksgiving **(Ezra 3:11).** Give thanks to the Lord and sing his praises because of his righteousness **(Psalm 7:17).** Give thanks to the Lord with all your heart and tell of all his wonderful deeds **(Psalm 9:1).**

Giving thanks in all circumstances is the most consistent guide of our spiritual health and wellness in Christ Jesus. Cultivating and maintaining an attitude of gratitude shows our appreciation and humility of both how unworthy we are before God and how kind and forgiving God is to us. For the LORD God is a sun and shield; the LORD bestows favor and honor; no good thing does he withhold from those whose walk is blameless **(Psalm 84:11).**

# SPECIAL ACKNOWLEDGEMENT

**I HEREBY ACKNOWLEDGE** a special friend, a sister, and an ardent supporter of my Grateful Soul Ministry. I met Mrs. Vivian Eneke Tataw Mambo in 1984 in the prestigious all girls boarding College (Our Lady of Lourdes College Mankon Bamenda) in Cameroon near the west coast of central Africa. We separated in 1987 and lost touch for an awfully long time.

By the special grace of God, we reconnected decades after in London United Kingdom in May of 2019! The royal reception she gave my girls and I was unforgettable! Her generosity left my children and I with grateful memories we will cherish forever! When we walked into her beautiful home, the calming spirit screamed the undeniable mighty presence of God in every corner of her house!

I have come to know, admire and cherish my beautiful and fearfully made friend and sister Vivian! She is a living example of a Proverbs 31 woman! She is a woman of Virtue. She is a woman after God's heart! She has faith in God and loves Jesus with all her heart! She is a loving mother to her children.

Her Faithfulness is portrayed in the love and trust her husband has for her. Her Reverence is displayed in the good things she brings to her husband and children. She is a good manager of her home. She is energetic and strong and makes sure her dealings are profitable to God and her family.

She is well rounded, great in the office and great in the kitchen. She is Charitable and extends a helping to those in need. She is a Provider. She is a wise steward of the gifts God has given her. She serves others with love and kindness.

am blessed and humbled to have her in my life as a sister and friend! I thank God for her life, and I bless her with every fiber of my being. May God almighty continue to bless, protect. and, provide for her and her family. When I pray for her and her family, I pray with joy! We give God all the glory!

# Other Books from the Gratitude Series

**My Letters of Gratitude to Jehovah God**

### Description

Evangeline N. Asafor is originally from Cameroon near the west coast of Central Africa. As a little girl growing up, she had a dream of one day becoming an international agent of social change—a dream she thought her native country could not contain. So, she migrated to the United States of America in October of 2000. One of her best days in America was the day she was sworn in as a US citizen! She made a promise to herself to be an asset to this great nation, not a liability. Evangeline has worked as a licensed practical nurse since 2004 in the areas of rehabilitation, hospice, and home health while attending school towards her greater passion of affecting social change as a criminal justice professional. One of Evangeline's worst moments in America happened when her husband was arrested for immigration irregularities, detained in Miami for eight months, and finally deported back to Cameroon.

The nightmares—and God's unending presence that followed these events—prompted the writing of Letters of Gratitude. Evangeline holds a master of science degree in criminal justice and is currently pursuing a Ph.D. degree in criminal justice at Walden University.

Features & details
Product information
Item Weight 10.7 ounces
Paperback 164 pages
ISBN-10 1947662074
ISBN-13 978-1947662070
Product Dimensions 6 x 0.37 x 9 inches
Customer Reviews 4.9 out of 5 stars 24Reviews
Publisher IEM PRESS (April 13, 2018)
Language: English

About the Kindle Edition
Length: 114 pages
Word Wise: Enabled
Screen Reader: Supported
Enhanced Typesetting: Enabled
Page Flip: Enabled
Description

Today it's been over three years since my sweet mother, Mama Philomena Mbuh Asafor, was called to be with Jehovah God. Though I miss her so much and will never fill the vacuum her death created in my life, her doctrines and life of godliness, gratitude, unconditional love, loyalty, struggles, integrity, resilience, and steadfastness are my vital tools for success.

Though I cannot see or touch her, I know she is near. As I listen with my heart, I can hear her love all around me so soft and clear. I will continue to keep my sweet mother's memories in my heart until I meet her again, nevermore to part.

It is well!

God gives, and God takes away. May Jehovah's name be glorified!

Features & details
Product Details
File Size: 3227 KB
Publication Date: August 9, 2018
Print Length: 114 pages
Publisher: IEM Press (August 9, 2018)
Language: English

## GRATITUDE AS A FACILITATOR OF OTHER VIRTUES IN JEHOVAH GOD

### Description

Gratitude as a virtue is incredibly significant in facilitating other virtues like Chastity, Charity, Diligence, Faith, Fortitude, Humility, Justice, Patience, Prudence, Temperance, and must be given the attention that it deserves. Gratitude is the quality of being thankful, readiness to show appreciation for and to return kindness. When gratitude is added as an ingredient to other virtues, it can increasingly benefit the soul and channel it to hunger and thirst for righteousness.

Features & details
Product information
Item Weight 9.3 ounces
Paperback 136 pages
ISBN-10 1947662406
ISBN-13 978-1947662407
Product Dimensions 6 x 0.31 x 9 inches
Customer Reviews 5.0 out of 5 stars 1Review
Publisher IEM PRESS (April 30, 2019)
Language: English

**GRATITUDE TO MY ANCESTORS ON WHOSE SHOULDERS I STAND TALL**

### Description

Thanks to the nourishment received from my rich cultural and spiritual roots supporting me, I humbly and proudly stand tall today. The wisdom that my ancestors shared generously has provided a shoulder and a platform on which I stand. I can never thank my ancestors enough for their crucial and meaningful contributions to my life as a village girl child raised on undisputed cultural and spiritual values. When I look back at my life growing up in a small African village and later moving into an all-girls boarding secondary school for five years under the guardianship of mostly Catholic nuns, an array of emotions come to me, from grateful tears, to sorrowful tears, and hearty laughter. The more I soul-search into the journey of ancestral wisdom that has brought me this far—from a small African village across the ocean to a town in America—the more grateful and empowered I feel in my God-ordained, purpose-driven life. It is important to celebrate my roots and my ancestors because they have nourished and defined the woman I am today.

Features & details
Product information
Item Weight 9.3 ounces
Paperback 188 pages
ISBN-10 1947662627
ISBN-13 978-1947662629
Product Dimensions 6 x 0.43 x 9 inches
Customer Reviews 5.0 out of 5 stars 4Reviews
Publisher IEM PRESS (November 9, 2019)
Language: English

## Gratitude to God When Family Rips Your Heart into a Million Little Pieces

**Description**

"The family has been defined as what the individual says it is. This may not necessarily be the one they were born into. Thus, being genetically related is hardly enough! Acceptance, compromise, gratitude, love, sacrifice, loyalty, respect, security, and trust are some of the things that create a family bond. Family betrayal is the ultimate wound that stings more than all others because it breaks a sacred code. It does not only rip your heart into a million little pieces, but it also darkens your soul. The pain of family betrayal is never forgotten and lingers like a fog in the depths of your soul. For all the modern-day Abels, Josephs, Jephthahs, Hagers, Ishmaels, Hoseas, and Tamars, I pray that your family betrayals, broken bonds, and unresolved differences reap the timely fruits of redemption, forgiveness, and healing in Jesus' name. Amen! "

Features & details
Product information
Item Weight 7.7 ounces
Paperback 158 pages

ISBN-10 1947662716
ISBN-13 978-1947662711
Product Dimensions 6 x 0.36 x 9 inches
Publisher IEM Press (May 30, 2020)
Language: English

# REFERENCES

The Holy Bible, New International Version : containing the Old Testament and the New Testament. (1984). International Bible Society. (Original work published 1973)

Baer D (2014). How 9 Incredibly Successful People Define Success retrieved from http://businessinsider.com/

*The Gandhi Message, Summer Solstice, Volume XXXVI, Number 2, 2002, Published by - The Mahatma Gandhi Memorial Foundation, Inc, Washington, D.C.20016*

6 Reasons why you must be prayerful by Apostle Joshua Selman. Retrieved from YouTube.com

www.ingramcontent.com/pod-product-compliance
Lightning Source LLC
Chambersburg PA
CBHW032257150426
43195CB00008BA/491